T0328513

The picture of the young boy in a remote and semi-desert area of Somaliland was taken by M. Abdulahi. It was taken while Mr Abdulahi was in Somaliland as a member of the team of International Election Observers for the 2010 Presidential Elections.This young boy stands alone in the empty plains, waiving the flag ofthe political party he is supposed to support.

This picture conveys the future challenges for Somaliland's political elite. The message says "do not forget us". All political parties have failed to bring young people into the fold, while democracy is the active participation of its citizens. There is a generation of young Somalilanders who are willing to get a response from their elected regarding their social daily life, and that demand participation in the political process of the nation

The photos here are published with permission

SOMALILAND: THE WAY FORWARD
Achieving its Rightful International Status

volume one

edited by
Jama Musse Jama

PONTE INVISIBILE
REDSEA-ONLINE.COM

To Ibrahim Megag Samatar, for his strong sense of duty, mission and personal sacrifice; for his passion and love for his country.

JMJ

REDSEA-ONLINE.COM Culture Foundation
Fidiyaha Aqoonta iyo Ereyga Dhigan - Xarunta dhexe
Daarta Oriental Hotel - Hargeysa, Somaliland
telephone: 00 252 2 525109
email: bookshop@redsea-online.com

Ponte Invisibile
Inquiries to the editor
Jama Musse Jama
Via Pietro Giordani 4, 56123 Pisa, Italy
www.ponteinvisibile.com
email: editor@redsea-online.com | editor@ponteinvisibile.com

Published by Ponte Invisibile (redsea-online), 2011, Pisa
I, II

Revised First Edition 2011
Copyright © Ponte Invisibile Edizioni 2011
A REDSEA-ONLINE Publishing Group Company.
ISBN 88-88934-18-9
EAN 9788888934181

Suggested classification for the librarians
Somaliland: the way forward - Achieving its Rightful International Status / Jama Musse
Jama (ed.)
p. 156, cm. 14.00 x 21.50
Includes Index.
ISBN 88-88934-18-9 EAN 9788888934181
I. Somaliland: the way forward - Achieving its Rightful International Status - Volume
one II. Jama Musse Jama (Jaamac Muuse Jaamac in Somali spelling) (edited by) III.
Contributed chapters; Somaliland Recognition.

CONTENTS

If there are dreams about a beautiful South Africa, there are also roads
that lead to their goal. Two of these roads could be named Goodness
and Forgiveness.
Nelson Mandela

FOREWORD

On May 18th, 1991, Somaliland embarked on a new path to decide on its own destiny as a sovereign state. For 20 years, since then, the people of Somaliland have demonstrated their strong commitment to achieving the goal of independence through democratic values and rejection of extremism. Since 1991 four peaceful and fair parliamentary and presidential elections, as well as a popular referendum were held. The local economy shows signs of hope, and the already announced forthcoming presence of international banks will further help Somaliland to trade with the world. In sum, Somaliland has successfully managed to overcome the aftermath of brutal war and the seeds sown by a brutal regime to build an enviable young thriving democracy dubbed by some as a beacon of stability and a model for Africa. Unfortunately, despite fulfilling all legal requirements for statehood, its search for sovereignty is yet to materialise. However, an encouraging sign of possible change to this situation is that in some part of the world, there is a growing sense of acknowledgement and contemplation that a revaluation of Somaliland case is necessary. Today, Somalilanders are looking back, with pride, at their achievements over the last 20 years; they will also be looking forward, with confidence, to face the challenges of fulfilling their dreams for an independent, peaceful and prosperous state. This book wants to draw lessons from that recent past, and intends to contribute the current debate within the regional and international community about the necessary political commitment to support the recognition of Somaliland, to support its people in realising their aspirations of achieving and cementing democracy and building an economically viability state, fully capable of gaining its rightful place in the international arena.

INTRODUCTION

Jama Musse Jama

Somaliland – the way forward is one part of a two-volume edition which is the result of a collaborative effort of several authors to document the recent advances in Somaliland in peace, development, good governance and economic revival. The two volumes have the ambitious goal of exploring a number of critical issues, including the state of law and order, justice and rights, national planning, democracy and political maturity, built on the centuries-old traditions of a nomadic Muslim society. They examine the role that those traditional approaches play in conflict management and resolution in the new Somaliland socio-political system. They will continue to play a significant role as society negotiates a peaceful and progressive path, reconciling the roles of clan, religion and gender, and allowing the structures of a new statehood to take root and to mature. The book delivers two core messages:

- That Somaliland recognition is both long overdue and essential for the consolidation of the continued peaceful evolution of a uniquely democratic state within the volatile East Africa region.
- That state-building is a product of the internal dynamics of a society which is possible even in the most precarious socio-economic settings; in other words, a politically sustainable path to stability and prosperity is the by-product of social self-regulation. In the case of Somaliland, this societal initiative is not, however, accompanied by a tangible political effort to promote the recognition of Somaliland.

The main goal of these two volumes, therefore, is to stimulate debate among scholars and policy-makers to create a platform for critical and innovative discourse around the themes of Somaliland recognition and state-building. The first volume presents an in-depth analysis of an emerging democracy in Africa, whereas the second volume presents a forward-looking analysis of the horizon with a view to offering recommendations for the way forward so that Somaliland leadership can meet the challenge of state capacity building.

The two complementary volumes, therefore, deliver two different but interconnected core messages. The first volume delivers a concise message about Somaliland's achievements and why it deserves international recognition, and what Somaliland and the world should do about the recognition issue. The second volume is about state-building and the future steps necessary for changes that the current and future governments of Somaliland must take to create the conditions for sovereign recognition. It is also expected that this book will help the international community to understand the reality on the ground and perhaps highlight gaps in the current knowledge of Somaliland, a new country which has, in many ways, already qualified itself as a viable democratic state fully deserving of formal international acceptance.

This first volume *"Achieving its Rightful International Status"* is dedicated to the late Ibrahim Megag Samatar, who was amongst the most influential of political thinkers of Somaliland, and includes also some of his major writings in which he eloquently defined his stand on the Somaliland issue and on the future of this nation. A true believer in Somaliland's nascent democracy and its future, Ibrahim Megag Samatar passed away this year (see Chapter 5 for details). He has been a central and very active participant in Somaliland politics for almost five decades, and his writings and political activism have significantly contributed to shaping the Somaliland identity.

In Chapter 1, H. E. Dr. Mohamed A Omar, the Foreign Minister of the Republic of Somaliland, provides a broad political, legal and historical basis for Somaliland's recognition, offering an answer as to why the international community should recognize Somaliland's statehood. He emphasizes how Somaliland already "acts as a state, maintains the security of its borders as a state, provides essential goods and services and represents an oasis of order and good governance in an unstable region"; he argues that "recognition would not only benefit Somaliland," but "it would also have a positive spill-over effect on the region and the wider world."

In Chapter 2, Sylvie Aboa-Bradwell, founder and director of the African Peoples Advocacy, UK, shows how, against all the odds and the expectations of regional and international communities, Somaliland has managed to deliver peace, security and several democratic governments to its people. She argues that "achieving statehood status will allow Somaliland to serve effectively as a democratic inspiration to African states and to Muslim nations all over the world."

In Chapter 3, Abdishakur Jowhar, a Somaliland political analyst, articulates a strong argument that the recognition of Somaliland is necessary if peace and prosperity are to come to the region. He argues that "Somaliland may fall victim to the unintended consequences of regional and international efforts directed at containing the Somali crisis." He believes that Somaliland has entered a new era "of imminent danger and immense opportunity." He comes to the conclusion that "Somaliland, acting under the umbrella and safety of international recognition, can dedicate itself to the process of finding a lasting solution to the Somali problem in a manner that no other nation can, with a dedication born out of self-interest and of the kinship it shares with all Somalis. Somaliland can bring together all Somalis to listen to the calls of life, liberty, peace and prosperity and to reject the calls of death, disorder and destruction as represented by Al Shabaab, by tribal forces and by Somali Piracy. Somaliland has the best chance of succeeding where others have failed. The unfortunate corollary to this is that Somalilanders do realize that without international recognition their perpetual fear of melting into the Somali crisis will come to pass. Somaliland has reached the proverbial fork in the road, a time for serious decisions. The world now needs Somaliland to come to its rescue just as Somaliland needs the world to come to its rescue and to that of its brethren the Somalis."

In Chapter 4, Michael Walls and Steve Kibble, joint coordinators of the 26 June 2010 Somaliland presidential international election observers, reiterate how the recent presidential elections have increased the likelihood that external powers will grant greater legitimacy to the state as donors. They underline how "powerful international actors seek to reward the country for a significant consolidation of past democratic gains," and they argue the existence of a potential for that role to be positive, "provided the Somaliland state proves itself capable of negotiating robustly and in the interests of a broad domestic polity."

Chapter 5 presents some of the writings of Ibrahim Megag Samatar, including his early political ideas, expectations and hopes as well as his demands for a democratic Somaliland. The chapter includes an unpublished work and two published articles of the late Professor Samatar, outlining his political vision for Somaliland. The second section of the chapter, which is based on an unpublished work, found by accident in his notes, is an extract of what is intended to become the first chapter of his forthcoming posthumous book. His daughter, Shukri, is collecting his notes, testifies how he "emphasizes the need for Somalilanders to look beyond the present difficulties in gaining international recognition and towards the future to consolidate the multi-party political system, so that the foundation of a sustainable democracy is firmly cemented."

The first volume concludes with an annotated bibliography on Somaliland which includes not only references cited for each chapter, but also other selected works relevant to Somaliland in general.

An overall message from this first volume is that Somaliland already enjoys all the prerequisite legal attributes of an independent state (see Chapter 1). However, it is not recognized as such because the international community lacks the political will. A generous reading would see this lack of will is largely to the result of a well-intentioned desire to allow Somaliland independence within the 'ideal' context of an 'all-parts-concerned' approach in which all the components of the former Somali Republic support independence of constituent parts through mechanisms such as referenda, as was the case in Eritrea and Southern Sudan. However, such an international and regional position, however well-intentioned, is not pragmatic and fatally ignores two undeniable facts: firstly, the Somaliland case is, as highlighted above, unique in that there is both a strong historical basis and earned legal rights for self-determination through a firmly established democratic process. Secondly, there is no apparent and sustainable solution to the crisis in Somalia in the near future which might lead to the establishment of a viable state and government there. The chances that a political entity able and willing to undertake direct discussions with Somaliland is therefore remote indeed. If not revisited, this entrenched lack of international political will would leave the future of millions of Somalilanders and Somalis more generally in the hands of warlords; individuals largely unwilling and/or incapable of serving the interests of their communities. This eventuality would perpetuate instability in the region and beyond. The core message of this volume, therefore, is, as noted in the first chapter, "to appeal to the regional and international leaders' common sense to adopt a pragmatic approach to the former Somali Republic politics, and within this framework recognize Somaliland as an independent state which has to be welcomed as the 55th member state of the AU."

CHAPTER 1

Recognizing Somaliland: Political, Legal and Historical Perspectives

Mohamed A Omar (PhD), Foreign Minister of Somaliland

"It is a deep irony that Somaliland – which has many of the empirical attributes of a state – has no legal status or representation in international fora, while Somalia – despite the absence of effective government since 1991 – continues to be accorded de jure sovereignty, with the TNG and TFG purporting to represent all the peoples of Somalia in a number of international bodies".[1] On 18 May 2011, Somaliland will mark 20 years of independence. Though a stable and functioning democracy, Somaliland has not been recognised by the international community. Instead it is still considered part of Somalia, which has remained in lawlessness and anarchy and is regarded as a failed state. In this chapter I examine the historical and legal basis for Somaliland's claim to be recognized as an independent state and explain the advantages that recognition would bring to Somaliland, the Horn of Africa region, and the wider world.

1. The Rise of Independent Somaliland

Before the colonial era, no formal, centralised state structures existed in the Horn of Africa. A decentralised system of clan-based administration and leadership among the Somali people, who possessed a common language, culture and religion, was the basis for governance and political expression.[2]

During the 'scramble for Africa' in the 19th century, European powers gradually colonised the region. As a result, the Somali

---

[1] Bradbury, M. (2008): *Becoming Somaliland*. Oxford: James Currey, pp. 5-6.
[2] See e.g. Touval S. (1963): *Somali Nationalism – International Politics and the Drive for Unity in the Horn of Africa*, Chapter 3. Cambridge: Harward University Press.

nation was divided among five colonial entities: the Italian Somaliland which in early 1950s attained self-rule under the UN Trusteeship as Somalia with its capital in Mogadishu; French Somaliland, now Djibouti; British Somaliland , now the Republic of Somaliland; the southernmost Somali communities which became part of Kenya under British rule; and the Somali region in the west which became part of Ethiopia. The colonial borders, blind to the Somali ethnicity, divided this nomadic, pastoral society between empires as has been done in other part of the world.

The colonial powers ruled with very different styles. Italy restructured the social hierarchy in Italian Somaliland (herein after refferred to as Somalia), disrupting historic clan ties.[3] By contrast British Somaliland was a protectorate and never fully colonised, interference with clan structures was minimal and the region was administered with a lighter touch. Britain's main interest was to facilitate the supply of meat to Aden via Berbera, whereas Italy invested in agriculture. These differing experiences affected the cohesion and subsequent direction of the two colonies.

After World War II a period of rapid decolonisation began. In 1950 Italy withdrew from Italian Somaliland while maintaining, for a period, an administrative role through the UN trusteeship of Somalia .[4] On 26 of June 1960, Britain granted Somaliland independence. For five days Somaliland existed as an independent, sovereign state. Somaliland then chose to unite with Somalia in pursuit of the elusive dream of a 'Greater Somalia' which would have united all Somali communities - Northern Kenya, Italian Somaliland, Eastern Ethiopia, British Somaliland and French Somaliland - based on the claim that such a nation had existed until the 19th century.[5]

---

[3] See e.g. Tripodi, P. (1999): *The Colonial Legacy in Somalia: Rome and Mogadishu: from Colonial Administration to Operation Restore Hope.* New York: St. Martin's Press.
[4] UN GA-Res. 289 (IV), 21 November 1949.
[5] See e.g.: Bayne, E.A. (1963): *Brinkmanship on the Horn: Somali Irredentism Remains a Perilous Factor in Eastern Africa.* American Universities Field Staff.

The Act of Union and the proclamation of the Somali Republic were, however, not formally signed by the parties involved.[6] Prior to unification, the Somalia and Somaliland legislatures had approved two separate Acts of Union. There was considerable disagreement over what the Act should contain, and the new National Assembly in Mogadishu approved it retrospectively. This, and the new constitution based upon the supposed Act of Union, received much criticism in the former British Somaliland, but any discontent was drowned by euphoria for unification.[7]

Initially there was great hope that an independent Somali Republic would forge a peaceful, united Somali culture, but illusions of harmony soon evaporated. Mogadishu became the country's capital, socio-economic development was focussed on the Somalia and all key positions in the government and military were awarded to southern Somalis, and so Somaliland (the north) found itself in political and economic isolation.[8]

The unequal situation became further pronounced when Mohamed Siad Barre seized power in a bloodless coup in 1969 and built a large and powerful army with the help of the Soviet Union. When Soviet support suddenly shifted to Ethiopia during the Ogaden War (1977), the United States rushed to fill the gap, providing substantial aid to Barre's regime despite widespread human rights abuse and Siad Barre's position as a military dictator.

Famine after the Ogaden War led to growing discontent with Barre's leadership and the formation of several opposition movements, including particularly the Somali National Movement (SNM), formed mainly from the Isaaq, the dominant clan in Somaliland. Barre saw the Isaaq, in particular, as a threat

---

[6] See e.g.: Rajagopal, B. and Carroll, A. J. (1992-1993): *The Case for the Independent Statehood of Somaliland.* American University Journal of International Law & Policy, Vol. 8, pp. 653-681.

[7] Schoiswohl, M. (2004): *Status and (Human Rights) Obligations of Non-Recognized De Facto Regimes in International Law.* University of Michigan: Martinus Nijhoff Publishers, pp. 112-115.

[8] See e.g. Adam, H. (1994): *Formation and Recognition of New States: Somaliland in Contrast to Eritrea.* Review of African Political Economy, No.59, Vol.2, p. 24.

to his regime. He responded to the formation of the SNM with severe measures aimed at weakening the clan in the north. He bombed and shelled Hargeysa, the north's capital, killing many civilians and reducing the city to rubble. His government also conducted ethnic cleansing of members of the Isaaq clan.

Siad Barre was overthrown in 1991 and Somalia was pitched into a state of anarchy. Twenty years later, all attempts to re-establish central government have failed despite a UN peacekeeping mission, UNOSOM II, which was established by UN Security Council Resolution 814 in 1993, and more recently the African Union Mission in Somalia (AMISOM), approved by the AU in January 2007 and endorsed the following month by UN Security Council Resolution 1744.

Meanwhile, the Republic of Somaliland declared its independence from the Somali Republic on 18 May 1991. Leaders of the SNM and elders of northern clans met at the 'Grand Conference of the Northern Peoples' in Burao. They officially revoked the 1960 Act of Union and adopted the borders of the former British Protectorate.[9]

This is not the place to discuss the long, difficult but ultimately successful process through which Somaliland progressed in order to achieve internal peace and stability and establish a democracy. However it is worth noting that on 31 May 2001, 97.9 per cent of Somaliland's population voted in favour of a new constitution, in a referendum endorsed by international observers as free and fair. As a gauge of support for the newly independent Somaliland and of the population's desire for self-determination, this result demonstrates an overwhelming majority is in favour of independence. Moreover, local elections took place in 2002, Presidential elections in 2003 and 2010, and parliamentary elections in 2005.

---

[9] Schoiswohl, M. (2004): *Status and (Human Rights) Obligations of Non-Recognized De Facto Regimes in International Law*. University of Michigan: Martinus Nijhoff Publishers, p. 116.

2. Somaliland's Legal Claim to Statehood

To assess Somaliland's legal claim to statehood, we should consider both its historical case and its demonstration of the attributes of statehood, as defined in international law.

Historical case

Somaliland's claim for independence is based primarily on historic title – its separate colonial history, a brief period of independence in 1960, the fact that it voluntarily entered into its unhappy union with Somalia and the questionable legitimacy of the 1960 Act of Union.[10] Unlike some other secessionist claims, Somaliland's independence does not violate the principle of uti possidetis. In 1964, the Organisation of African Unity resolved that the principle of uti possidetis – that former colonial borders should be maintained upon independence – should be adhered to in the interests of stability of borders. The principle is also enshrined in the Constitutive Act of the African Union. Somaliland's independence therefore restores the colonial borders of the former British Protectorate of Somaliland.

The separation of fused states into their former territories has precedents in Africa: Egypt and Syria were joined as the United Arab Republic (UAR) from 1958-1961; the failed Fédération du Mali united Senegal and Mali for just over a year in 1960; the Sénégambia Confederation was the result of a brief merging of the now separate countries of Senegal and Gambia; and Eritrea separated from Ethiopia in 1991.[11]

---

[10] Rajagopal, B. and Carroll, A. J. (1992-1993): *The Case for the Independent Statehood of Somaliland.* American University Journal of International Law & Policy, Vol. 8, pp. 653-681.

[11] See respectively Jankowski, J. (2002): Nasser's Egypt, Arab Nationalism, and the United Arab Republic. Boulder: Lynne Rienner; Kienle E. (1995): Arab Unity Schemes Revisited: Interest, Identity, and Policy in Syria and Egypt. International Journal of Middle East Studies, Vol.27, p. 53; Kurtz, D. M. (1970): Political Integration in Africa: The Mali Federation. Journal of Modern African Studies, Vol.8, Issue 3, p. 405; Cutter, C. H. (1966): Mali: A Bibliographical Introduction. African Studies Bulletin No.9, p.74; Richmond, E. B. (1993): Senegambia and the Confederation: History, Expectations, and Disillusions. Journal of Third World Studies, Vol.X, No.1, p. 172; and Jacquin-Berdal, D. (2002): Nationalism

Britain granted and recognized the independence of Somaliland in 1960. Somaliland then voluntarily opted for unification with Somalia to form the Somali Republic. Having entered voluntarily into an unhappy union, Somaliland must also be allowed to withdraw, as others have before.[12]

The validity of the Act of Union is anyway unclear. In June 1960, representatives from Somaliland and Somalia each signed different Acts of Union, and therefore agreed to different terms of unification; the official Act of Union was passed retrospectively in January 1961 by the new National Assembly, and in a referendum on the new Constitution of the Somali State, held in June 1961, an extremely low turnout in Somaliland (less than one sixth of the population), and an overwhelming rejection of the document by those who voted, demonstrated discontent with the union. [13]

The 1960 unification of Somalia and Somaliland failed to meet domestic or international legal standards for treaty formation, and the Act of Union falls short of the Vienna Convention's legal requirements for a valid international treaty. The union has essentially been secured by recognition alone.[14]

Attributes of Statehood

The main criteria for statehood remain those set by the 1933 Montevideo Convention, generally considered a norm of customary international law:

"The State as a person of international law should possess the following qualifications:
(a) a permanent population;
(b) a defined territory;

---

and Ethnicity in the Horn of Africa: A Critique of the Ethnic Interpretation. Lewiston: The Edwin Mellen Press, Chapter 3, p. 79.

[12] Mazrui, A. A. (2006): Africa's Bondage of Boundaries: Can the Shackles Be Loosened? Public lecture delivered on the 22 March at Hargeysa University under the chairmanship of the President of the University, Hargeysa, Somaliland.

[13] See e.g. Drysdale, J. (1991): Somaliland: The Anatomy of Secession. London: Haan Associates.

[14] Vienna Convention on the Law of Treaties (1969).

(c) government; and
(d) capacity to enter into relations with the other states."[15]
Somaliland unequivocally meets each of these established legal criteria.

a. A permanent population

The population of the Republic of Somaliland is estimated to be approximately 3.5 million. As with its neighbours, a large proportion of the population are nomadic, and movement of people through porous borders in the Horn of Africa region is commonplace; but this does not affect any questions of permanency or existence of population as defined in international law.

b. A defined territory

Somaliland's territory is clearly defined as that of the former British protectorate, established by treaties in the late 19th century and reaffirmed when Somaliland acquired independence in 1960. Although the eastern frontier has been contested, „border disputes do not in general invalidate statehood".[16]

c. Effective government

Somaliland has a functioning central government which exercises effective control over the majority of its territory. It has had several sets of elections deemed free and fair by international observers , most recently in June 2010, when observers praised presidential elections as a "peaceful expression of the popular will".[17] It has set up governmental institutions including a constitution approved by a popular vote, a democratically elected President, national parliament, local governments, and an independent judiciary.

---

[15] Montevideo Convention on the Rights and Duties of States, 1933, Article 1.
[16] Schoiswohl, M. (2004): *Status and (Human Rights) Obligations of Non-Recognized De Facto Regimes in International Law*. University of Michigan: Martinus Nijhoff Publishers, p. 166.
[17] See Progressio Press Release, 28 June 2010, http://www.progressio.org.uk/blog/news/somaliland-elections-peaceful-expression-popular-will.

d. Capacity to enter into relations with other States

Somaliland has entered into formal and informal arrangements with a wide variety of states and intergovernmental organisations. Its representatives in the United Kingdom, Sweden, the United States, Djibouti, Ethiopia and Kenya deal with their host governments. Due to its unrecognised status, Somaliland suffers limitations in the diplomatic sphere which adversely affect its ability to deliver political and economic benefits to its people. Somaliland already enjoys a de facto recognition among many nations around the world.

Although Somaliland fulfills all "the normative criteria of statehood as they have traditionally been applied in international law"[18], its efforts to achieve recognition as an independent state have been largely unsuccessful. This is because such recognition is essentially a political act, not a legal one. The advancement of Somaliland's case is dependent upon the will of the international community – something which, as yet, has been lacking. Thus the Republic of Somaliland remains in limbo. It acts as a state, maintains the security of its borders as a state, provides essential goods and services and represents an oasis of order and good government in an unstable area. I will argue that recognition would not only benefit Somaliland, it would also have a positive effect on the region and the wider world.

3. How recognition would improve the economic situation of Somaliland and the region

Non-recognition imposes significant costs on Somaliland. For example, under the 1982 UN Convention on the Law of the Sea, a state has special rights to exploit marine resources in an exclusive economic zone (EEZ) up to 200 nautical miles from its coast.[19] As

---

[18] Yannis, A. (2000): *State Collapse and the International System – Implosion of Government and the International Legal Order from the French Revolution to the Disintegration of Somalia.* Geneva: IUHEI, p.129.

[19] See articles 56 & 57 of the Convention.

an unrecognized state, Somaliland is unable to declare an EEZ off its 850 km long coast line, and foreign fishing companies can pillage Somaliland fish stocks with impunity. The fishing sector's potential is high, despite its current underdeveloped state.[20]

Somaliland is not a signatory of the 1944 Convention on International Civil Aviation (the Chicago Convention); it was the Somali Republic which signed the agreement in June 1964. This makes it harder for Somaliland to regulate the use of its airspace.[21] It is also difficult for Somaliland to negotiate bilateral air services agreements and collect over-flight fees from foreign aircrafts that overfly its territory. Non-recognition complicates insurance coverage as foreign vessels wanting to use the port of Berbera must pay higher insurance premiums[22] - which in turn make it harder to attract foreign direct investment (FDI).

Non-recognition also increases the perception of risk on the part of companies which might do business in Somaliland, as it is seen as being part of Somalia, the archetypal failed state.

In addition, non-recognition has limited access to foreign aid, which tends to be channeled through multilateral agencies and focused in humanitarian rather than developmental needs; international political sensitivies over Somaliland's status have meant that very little assistance has been directed to support the building of government institutions.[23]

An internationally recognized Somaliland would benefit from stronger bilateral aid flows and increased FDI. This would strengthen Government revenue, which would allow the central administration to deliver better basic services - water supply, education, health care, and infrastructure. More FDI would create jobs, improve competition, promote economic diversification

---

[20] Agaloglou, M. (2011): Somaliland: past, Present and Future. Think Africa Press, Part 10, http://thinkafricapress.com/somalia/somaliland-past-present-and-future-part-10.

[21] Article 1 of the Chicago Convention: "The contracting States recognize that every State has complete and exclusive sovereignty over the airspace above its territory".

[22] Bradbury, M. (2008): *Becoming Somaliland*. Oxford: James Currey, p. 154.

[23] Bradbury, M. (2008): *Becoming Somaliland*. Oxford: James Currey, p. 158.

and thus contribute to the welfare of Somaliland's people and to stability.

A fully recognized Somaliland would also be of benefit for the region as a whole, contributing to the economic development of the Horn and becoming an important commercial centre of strategic significance and a gateway to the Gulf countries.

Full diplomatic relations with Ethiopia would allow formal transit agreements, improving access to the sea for this land-locked country, which has a population of over 80 million and whose economy is growing annually at around 7%.[24] Approximately 65% of imports through Berbera are already destined for Ethiopia.[25] Recognition would encourage investment in the Berbera port itself as well as the potential construction of a railway and further investment along the Berbera corridor, an 850km long road which connects Ethiopia's capital Addis Ababa to Berbera. Recognition would foster improvements of regional transport infrastructure, for example the Berbera corridor. It would also permit better telecommunications links in the Horn of Africa.

4. A fully recognized Somaliland as an anchor for political stability and security in the Horn

Somaliland has, largely through its own efforts, become an area of relative peace and stability in a region plagued by the collapse of governmental authority, terrorism, and piracy. Over the past 20 years, the international community has generally neglected Somaliland while concentrating on trying to find a solution to the failed state of Somalia. This penalizes Somaliland for successfully establishing democracy, peace and rule of law. The TFG as Somalia's formal representative at international fora and towards the international community is in the position to divert diplomatic and financial resources intended for

---

[24] CIA World Factbook (2011), https://www.cia.gov/library/publications/the-world-factbook/geos/et.html (figures for 2010).
[25] Agaloglou, M. (2011): Somaliland: past, Present and Future. Think Africa Press, Part 9, http://thinkafricapress.com/somalia/somaliland-past-present-and-future-part-9.

Somaliland. "As the territorial definition of the Somali state is recognized in preference to the existing political authorities … the borders of Somalia remain the reference point for the policies of the UN and other international bodies".[26]

Somaliland today must defend its people and its democracy against the threat of terrorism and extremism in general at great cost. It cooperates willingly with its neighbours and the wider international community – in the fight against terrorism by exchanging information about potential threats, enforcing the UN arms embargo against Somalia and policing its own territory. Somaliland continues to arrest and imprison pirates who break Somaliland laws. The waters off Somaliland's coast are largely free from pirate attacks, and nearly 90 pirates are in prison in Hargeysa.

An internationally recognized Somaliland would be more than ready to share its experiences on internal and local conflict resolution, peace and nation building. Somaliland is an example of what can be achieved in the same cultural context as a contribution towards the search for peace and democracy in Somalia as well as in the region as a whole.

Being in the frontline of the fight against piracy, terrorism and extremism, a fully recognized and better resourced Somaliland would be able to become a more effective buffer against piracy, terrorism and extremism in the region, and a more capable partner within IGAD and the African Union on security issues.

5. The AU's Position

An AU Commission visited Somaliland in 2005 and concluded that the AU "should be disposed to judge the case of Somaliland from an objective historical viewpoint and a moral angle vis-à-vis the aspirations of the people".[27] Somaliland accordingly applied

---

[26] Bradbury, M. (2008): Becoming Somaliland. Oxford: James Currey, pp. 5-6 and p. 200.
[27] African Union Commission (2005) Resume: AU Fact-Finding Mission to Somaliland (30 April to 4 May 2005).

to join the AU in 2005, but the application is still pending. Some AU members are apparently worried about the precedent which recognizing Somaliland would set for other African nations which contain substantial ethnic minorities inside borders which were originally drawn by the European powers. However, South Sudan voted overwhelmingly for independence in a referendum on 9 January 2011 and it appears that AU member states are likely to recognize it, allowing it to become the 54th member state of the AU. Furthermore, there is no real reason why states outside Africa should not recognize Somaliland now regardless of the position of the AU.

6. Conclusion

Somaliland enjoys all the legal attributes of an independent state. It is not recognized as such because the international community lacks the political will. I would like to appeal to the world, and especially our brothers in Africa, to set aside their reservations and recognize Somaliland as an independent state and welcome it as the 55th member state of the AU. An internationally recognized Somaliland would contribute to the stability, security and prosperity of the Horn of Africa as well as helping to defeat evils such as piracy in the Indian Ocean. The true interests of the international community would best be served by recognizing Somaliland now.

CHAPTER 2

An Unsung African Marvel:
The Case for Somaliland's Recognition

Sylvie Aboa-Bradwell

Introduction

There is an African state offering its people democracy, peace and security in a war-torn part of Africa. Several elections, including two presidential elections, widely acknowledged as free and fair by international observers, have been held there peacefully . None of its presidents has sought to alter the constitution in order to perpetuate his tenure, as has happened in countless African states. Furthermore, this country's incumbent president was recently defeated by one of the opposition candidates. He did not attempt to discredit the election or resort to intimidation and violence to cling to power, as Robert Mugabe of Zimbabwe, Mwai Kibaki of Kenya and Laurent Gbagbo of Côte d'Ivoire, to name but a few, have done. Instead, he graciously congratulated his opponent and, in accordance with the constitution, relinquished power 30 days after the election.

This state could serve as an inspiration not only to the African continent, but also to the whole world. Within a few years, it has managed to accomplish a feat that has seemingly eluded almost all African states for decades, since their so-called independence. It has incorporated key elements of traditional African structures of government into a modern democratic system based on free and fair elections. In so doing, this country has, on the one hand, enabled its people to hold their rulers accountable and control them through democracy. On the other hand, it has allowed different clans and ethnic communities to co-exist peacefully by resorting to effective, centuries-old African conventions to resolve grievances and differences that mere elections, however free and fair, would not settle otherwise. As its population is almost entirely Muslim, this state is in a position to show the whole world that democracy and Islam are far from being incompatible.

An African state that not only Africa, but also the whole world could look up to? This statement may seem laughable. Unsurprisingly, most people are reluctant to believe that such a marvel could possibly exist. This state is not recognised by any other state in the world. Instead of being congratulated for its unique, extraordinary achievements, it is being shunned and derided. Instead of being hailed as a peace haven and a precious islet of democracy in a sea of bloody dictatorships and covert tyrannies, this state is being ostracised. The state in question is called or rather, more accurately, calls itself the Republic of Somaliland.

This paper examines and refutes the most common objections to Somaliland's recognition. It argues that the African Union, Western nations, and the international community should support the independence of this territory without delay. Such a stance will act as a catalyst for economic development in Somaliland, and will give this state the stature it needs to operate as a unique democratic role model for African and other countries.

Somaliland women queuing to vote at the 2010 election

Somaliland men queuing to vote at the 2010 election

Analysis and Refutation of the Objections to Somaliland's Recognition

One of the main reasons often given to justify the non-recognition of Somaliland as a state is the fear of opening the floodgates by recognising a breakaway region of a sovereign nation, thus threatening the integrity of every nation in the world.[28] Those who use this argument fail to acknowledge that the recognition of Croatia, Serbia, Macedonia and all the other states that declared themselves independent following the collapse of Yugoslavia did not lead to the disintegration of other countries all over the world. Nobody can seriously believe that the acceptance of one African state is likely to have more repercussions around the world than the recognition of nearly ten newly formed European countries.

As so often when dealing with African issues, some people may be tempted to use double standards. They may argue that the African context is so different, or that the situation is so volatile

---

[28] See, for instance, Abdulkadir Mohamoud, "Somalia: Why Somaliland Is not Kosovo: the case of the failed recognition", Horseed Media (12 August 2010), retrieved online on 2 January 2011 http://www.horseedmedia.net/2010/08/12/somaliland-is-not-osovo/.

in the Horn of Africa that the status quo is better than the many problems that the recognition of Somaliland could trigger. It would certainly be very easy for superficial observers of African affairs to cite the countless civil wars that have ravaged African countries in order to justify the view that separatist aspirations should not be encouraged in this continent.

But Africans are not intrinsically more war-prone than other human beings. An in-depth analysis of these African conflicts reveals that almost all of them were either direct consequences or by-products of the Cold War policies that had transformed Africa into the playground of the Soviet Union, the United States and their respective allies. Now that the international circumstances that did wreak so much havoc on Africa have changed, a new, bold, imaginative approach to African problems is required from Africans, Westerners, and the international community in general.

Although Somaliland submitted its application for recognition as a state to the African Union (AU) in 2005, this organisation has not yet processed the said application. Such an attitude is mainly attributable to the AU's desire to maintain the borders inherited by African countries from Western colonisers. Bearing in mind that these borders were designed with total disregard for ethnic, religious, linguistic or cultural divisions, it is certainly true that many African states could collapse if the secessionist desires of these heterogeneous groups were actively encouraged.

But Somaliland is not seeking independence from Somalia on the grounds of ethnic, religious, linguistic or cultural differences. Somali people are mainly united, not divided by these elements. In an ideal world, they would all be living in a single African state. But in the real world, they are already living not only in Somalia, but also in different African countries, including Ethiopia, Djibouti and Kenya. They were divided, not by the aspirations of Somaliland, but by historical and external circumstances beyond their control. The notion of Greater Somalia is now widely acknowledged by most Somalis as a dangerous chimera.

Ironically, in accordance with the AU's principle of preserving the borders bequeathed by former colonisers, Somaliland has an undeniable claim to statehood: when it obtained independence from British colonial rule on 26th June 1960, Somaliland was recognised as a sovereign state not only by the United Nations but also by more than thirty countries. Somaliland decided to join the former UN Trust Territory of Somalia (which was formerly Italian Somalia) on 1st July 1960 to form a new entity called the Somali Republic. This was believed to be the first step of the unification of all the Somalis in the Horn of Africa under one state, .[29]

The problems and divisions confronting the union from the onset, the marginalisation of Somaliland people, the destruction of Somaliland by the dictatorial regime of Siad Barre, the popular uprisings by the people of Somaliland, and the all-community conferences which approved the decision to withdraw from the union on 18th May 1991, are all well known and equally well documented.[30] This was followed by resolute steps towards democracy culminating in a series of democratic elections. For instance, there was a referendum on the new Somaliland constitution in 2001; municipal elections were held in 2002, 2003 and 2009; parliamentary elections took place in 2005, while presidential elections were held in 2005 and 2010.

The legal rules that were applied to the Gambia when it was recognised as a state after its secession from Senegal in 1989 should also be applicable to Somaliland. The argument that the Horn of Africa's territories should be treated differently because

---

[29] Some Somalilanders use this as a basis to argue that strictly speaking, Somaliland did never become part of a country called Somalia but instead there has been a merge of Somaliland and Somalia to form the Republic of Somalia as the first stone of "Greater Somali Nation" which is a failed project.

[30] An excellent historical overview of the union between Somaliland and the former Italian Somalia, and the emergence of Somaliland, is provided by Franco Henwood in "A Contribution to the Case for Somaliland's Recognition", Holler Africa, originally published in the November/ December 2006 edition of African Renaissance, retrieved on 2 January 2011 http://www.hollerafrica.com/showArticle.php?artId=202&catId=1. A report from Kenya's members of parliament fact finding mission to Somaliland in December 2006 also provides very insightful background information. It is available online on Somaliland Patriots, retrieved on 2 January 2011 http://www.somalilandpatriots.com/news-2898-0.

of the volatility of this region does not stand up to scrutiny. The international recognition of Eritrea's independence from Ethiopia in 1993 did not lead to an avalanche of applications for statehood recognition from neighbouring territories.

The AU itself acknowledges that sticking to the ironclad maxim of the inviolability of borders inherited from colonialism would be neither wise nor appropriate in the case of Somaliland. The report of an AU fact finding mission to Somaliland between 30th April and 4th May 2005 states that this territory's "case should not be linked to the notion of 'opening a Pandora's box'. As such, the AU should find a special method for dealing with this outstanding case"; and adds, "The lack of recognition ties the hands of the authorities and people of Somaliland, as they cannot effectively and sustainably transact with the outside to pursue the reconstruction and development goals." [31] The obvious question is why, almost five years later, the AU has not yet acted upon these bold and judicious recommendations.

Despite its acknowledgement of the special circumstances of Somaliland, as well as the negative impact of the lack of recognition on the people of Somaliland, the AU has not yet attempted to end the status quo because it is still hell-bent on pursuing its long-standing policy of following the diktat of the international community or rather, more accurately, the diktat of Western nations. In 2006, the AU agreed to support the Western-backed invasion of Somalia by Ethiopian troops in order to oust the Islamic Courts (IC) and strengthen the control of the country by the Transitional Federal Government (TFG). This was not an action demanded or approved by the Somali people. It was mainly triggered by United States' perception of the IC as hostile Islamic terrorists. The subsequent splintering of the IC into several armed factions opposed to the TFG, the emergence of the radical organisation Al-Shabaab, the continuous meddling

---

[31] Cited by Jean-Jacques Cornish in "AU Supports Somalia Split", *Mail & Guardian Online* (2006), retrieved on 2 January 2011 http://www.mg.co.za/article/2006-02-10-au-supports-somali-split.

of the United States, Ethiopia, Eritrea and other countries, are only some of the factors that will make peace and stability elude Somalia for years, if not decades.

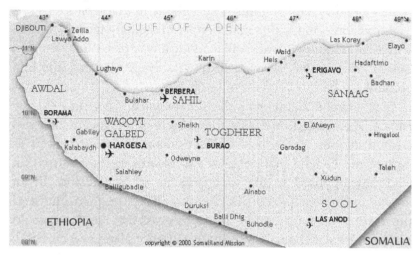

Map of Somaliland

Recommendations for the African Union

With nearly 10,000 of its troops operating in Somalia to prop up the Transitional Federal Government (TFG), the African Union is torn between its realization that Somaliland has a strong, legitimate claim to statehood recognition, and its support of the TFG, which is opposed to Somaliland's independence. The AU should stop dithering and take the lead in implementing the recommendations of its own fact finding mission to Somaliland. The reliance of the TFG on AU troops for its survival gives the AU an excellent bargaining chip. The AU can use these circumstances to initiate negotiations with Somalia, and strive to persuade this country to follow in the footsteps of Ethiopia by consenting to the independence of Somaliland just as Ethiopia consented to the independence of Eritrea in 1993.

When negotiating with Somalia, the AU should stress that it is absolutely not motivated by a desire to divide the Somali

people. The AU should make it clear that it is driven by the wish
to end the suffering of Somali communities. Somalia should be
convinced that clinging to Somaliland against the wish of most
of this territory's inhabitants is very likely to exacerbate tensions
and divisions amongst Somali people in the long term. Granting
Somaliland independence will provide a way of settling disputes
that if left unsolved now, will inevitably plunge Somalia and
Somaliland back into chaos in the future.

Somaliland's claim over the territories of Sool and eastern
Sanaag is contested by the Puntland State of Somalia, which was
created in 1998 and which, unlike Somaliland, regards itself as
part of the Federal State of Somalia. However, Puntland is not
viscerally opposed to the independence of Somaliland. In an
interview granted to the BBC in May 2006, the then Puntland
president, Mohamud "Adde" Muse, asserted that Puntland would
not interfere with Somaliland's independence plans, and declared:
"We hope they will work with us in a brotherly, Somali way."[32]

Furthermore, while the current president of Puntland,
Abdirahman Muhammad Farole, has expressed his desire to
control the disputed territories, the African Union is fully aware
that his government is far more preoccupied by security threats
from Al-Shabaab and piracy, and that the leaders and elites of the
disputed areas are now seeking to become autonomous.[33] The AU
is in a position to persuade Somaliland to take into consideration
the preoccupations of the people of these areas in exchange for
statehood recognition, and convince Puntland to drop its claim
over Sool and eastern Sanaag in exchange for the security that a
recognised, stable and peaceful Somaliland would guarantee. But
neither the AU nor any of the advocates of the union between
Somalia and Somaliland can persuade Somaliland's young
generations and future leaders to give up the independence of
their state. For they have never lived under the union, and for

---

[32] Cited in International Crisis Group, Somaliland: Time for African Union
Leadership, Africa Report No 110, 23 May 2006, p. 10.
[33] African Union, Report of the Chairperson of the Commission on the Situation
in Somalia, 8 January 2010, p. 7.

them, an independent Somaliland is an integral, non-negotiable part of their identity.

The AU should take the lead, and seek to convince Somalia that maintaining the status quo and carry on opposing the independence of Somaliland is not only merely postponing the unavoidable, but also holding the people of Somaliland hostage to the uncertain fate of Somalia. Furthermore, it is akin to inflicting a cruel, short-sighted collective punishment on Somalilanders, who are not responsible for the current sorry state of Somalia.

Some may argue that instead of seeking statehood recognition, Somaliland should merely administer itself while waiting for Somalia to be stabilised.[34] But they are missing a crucial point that the AU has already grasped: lack of recognition is preventing Somalilanders from exploiting their natural resources. Somaliland is ostracised, unrecognised by potential trade partners and investors, and unable to deal with institutions such as the International Monetary Fund or the World Bank. Consequently, though surveys have revealed that their country has mineral deposits, as well as many offshore and onshore oil and natural gas reserves, Somalilanders are forced to live in abject poverty, and rely only on livestock and remittances from the Diaspora. This situation was rightly deplored in 2009 by the then Somaliland foreign minister, Abdillahi Duale: "We rely on ourselves and our Diaspora, which accounts for almost $600m of revenue a year. People get by but it is very difficult without infrastructure," he pointed out before declaring, "We need butter, we are not asking for guns."[35]

The AU should seek to convince Somalia that consenting to the independence of Somaliland would not be a sign of weakness, but a wise move that would benefit not only Somalilanders, but also all Somali people in general. For the ties bounding Somali

---

[34] Abdulkadir Mohamoud, op cit.
[35] Quoted by James Melik in "Riches of Somaliland Remain Untapped", BBC News (15 March 2009), retrieved on 2 January 2011 http://news.bbc.co.uk/1/hi/business/7935139.stm.

communities transcend mere borders, and the benefits from an economic prosperity enjoyed by Somalilanders are likely to trickle down to other Somali people. Granting independence to Somaliland will provide this country with the tools that will enable it to show that when left alone, Somali people are capable of governing themselves in a peaceful and democratic way, eradicate corruption, manage their national wealth for the common good, and achieve economic prosperity.

It is true that the citizens of many African states with natural resources have not benefited from this wealth. But unlike these countries, before starting to exploit its resources, Somaliland has endowed itself with a social and political structure that will help prevent the rulers from embezzling public funds. The elected representatives of the lower house are accountable to the electors as well as the upper house, and the elders of the upper house are accountable to the members of their clans.

Inauguration of President Ahmed Mohamed Silanyo in July 2010

Democracy as a True African Form of Government

Democracy is a fragile, albeit precious commodity that needs concrete, tangible positive results to satisfy people's legitimate aspirations and in so doing, remain sustainable. Somaliland can consolidate its fledgling democracy by giving economic development to its people. The AU should champion international recognition as a way of boosting economic development in Somaliland. Such a stance would enable this organisation to show that it has the capacity to effectively tackle one of the main challenges facing the African continent in the 21st century: the need to rid itself of the failed, disastrous dictatorial system bequeathed and backed mainly by former Western colonisers throughout the 20th century, and embrace democracy as a true African form of government.

Expressions such as "African big men" and "African despots" are frequently used to refer to dictators like Mobutu Sese Seko of Zaire (now Democratic Republic of Congo) or Robert Mugabe of Zimbabwe, as if such tyrants were African idiosyncrasies. But far from being peculiar to African culture, these tyrants were often chosen and kept in power by Westerners who used them to control their former African colonies. As they did not enjoy the overwhelming support of their compatriots, these dictators had to resort to mass slaughter to crush dissidents. They did not hesitate to do so, safe in the knowledge that their Western allies would back them as long as they served Western interests. For instance, while he repeatedly carried out massacres in Matabeland in the 1980s, Mugabe was made a Knight Commander of the Order of the Bath on the advice of John Major's government in 1994.

Genuine African culture is intrinsically democratic. This is why in the past, most African communities had a place called "discussion tree", where chiefs and leaders would discuss important issues with their people, and consult them before acting. These rulers knew that they could not govern without popular approval, and that they had to prioritise the common good over their personal interests. By supporting democracy in Somaliland, the African Union would be letting tyrants such as Laurent Gbagbo and Robert Mugabe know that it could no longer allow them to use opportunistic, hypocritical anti-Western rhetoric and fake African nationalism to ignore the will of their people and perpetuate themselves in power. A genuine African leader would not have relied on French troops to quell an insurrection as Gbagbo did in 2002; it would not have been necessary for a ruler chosen by African people to sign the Lancaster House Agreement before obtaining power, as it was for Mugabe.[36]

The Need for Westerners to Support Democracy in Africa

This is the right time for the African Union to champion democracy in Africa, and make bad African leaders understand the following once and for all: wealth looted by African-born thieves is as needed by Africans as wealth taken by colonisers, and the lives of Africans slaughtered by African egomaniacs are as irreplaceable as the lives of Africans killed by foreigners. The time is ripe for such a stance because most Westerners are now prepared to let Africans choose their own leaders. They may not necessarily do so out of the belief that Africans can now rule themselves effectively, but because they realize that in a world increasingly dominated by China and other non-Western nations, they can no longer impose their will on other people in a blatant way. Nevertheless, the most important thing is that most Africans currently have a unique opportunity to turn their backs on decades of autocratic rule that had given them nothing but untold suffering and abject poverty.

Given the spectacular economic development of dictatorial China, some Africans may be tempted to argue that African nations should imitate the Chinese and prioritise economic development over democracy. But alongside the African Union and the advocates of Africa's democratisation, the West is in an ideal position to produce a powerful counter-narrative that

---

[36] This was the agreement of independence of Rhodesia, now Zimbabwe, from the United Kingdom. It was signed in Lancaster House, London, in December 1979, following negotiations between parties including the British government, the Rhodesia government and the Patriotic Front led by Robert Mugabe and Joshua Nkomo.

will resonate throughout Africa for the foreseeable future: dictatorship is a form of government alien to Africans that has already repeatedly failed to deliver economic prosperity in Africa. African ways, lifestyle and values are closer to the Western rather the Chinese model. As George Ayittey rightly put it:

The Chinese communist model is fundamentally alien to indigenous Africa. [...] Africa's salvation lies in returning to its roots and building upon its own indigenous heritage of free village markets, free enterprise, free trade and participatory democracy based upon consensus.[37]

By consenting to proposals for a democratic, independent Botswana in 1964, the British showed that Westerners could support Africa's return to its democratic roots. The proof that democracy is the way forward for Africa is that in terms of impressive economic development, peace and stability, Botswana is one of the very few African success stories. But it is extremely difficult, if not impossible for the rest of African countries to emulate this model: decades of tyrannical rule and injustice have created an explosive climate of ethnic, religious or cultural tensions, resentment and confrontation that does not exist in Botswana. This is why the case of Somaliland's democracy is particularly useful.

The African Union, Western nations and the international community should support Somaliland's democratic form of government as a successful model that can and should be replicated all over the African continent. As stated earlier, Somaliland's formula of adopting free and fair elections as well as elements of traditional African structures of government allows divided communities to overcome problems that cannot be solved through elections alone. The recognition of Somaliland as a state will end the international community's tendency to

---

[37] George Ayittey, "*Economist* Debates: Africa and China, The Opposition's Rebuttal Remarks", *The Economist* (17th February 2010), retrieved on 2 January 2011 http://www.economist.com/debate/days/view/467.

associate this territory with the on-going Somali chaos. This will give Somaliland the respect, exposure and platform it needs to stop being an unsung African marvel, and function as a role model for African as well as other nations.

Conclusion

There is a pressing need for the recognition of Somaliland. The most common objection to the acknowledgement of this territory, namely that such a move would jeopardise the integrity of African as well as other states, does not stand up to scrutiny. The volatility of the Horn of Africa, the past African civil wars, and the Puntland claim over the territories of Sool and eastern Sanaag soley based on kinship cannot justify the status quo either. Opposing the independence of Somaliland is merely postponing the unavoidable, as an independent state is now a non-negotiable part of the identity of Somaliland's young generations and future leaders. Furthermore, factors such as the incapacity of the Transitional Federal Government to defeat the various armed factions opposed to it, the strengthening of Al-Shabaab and the interference of many interested countries and groups, will keep peace and stability at bay in Somalia for the foreseeable future. Continuing to view and treat Somaliland as a region of Somalia is tantamount to holding Somaliland people hostage to Somalia's troubled fate, and inflicting an unfair collective punishment on them.

Against all the odds and expectations, Somaliland has managed to deliver peace, security and several democratic governments to its people. The African Union, Western nations and the international community should show their admiration for these accomplishments and seek to safeguard them by recognising Somaliland as an independent state. This will prove immensely beneficial not only to Somaliland people, but also to African nations as well as the international community as a whole. Recognition will enable Somaliland to increase the exploitation of its resources and offer economic prosperity to its citizens. Achieving statehood status will also allow Somaliland to serve effectively as a democratic inspiration to African states and to Muslim nations all over the world.

CHAPTER 3

Somaliland Recognition- a Rational Solution to the Somali Crisis

Abdishakur A Jowhar

A reflective mood

Somalilanders are in a reflective mood as they prepare for the 20th Anniversary of the birth of their nation. These days there is a sense of contemplation, thoughtfulness and revaluation in Somaliland circles.

It is in this context that Jama Musse Jama has initiated a process of contemplation that can transform this reflection into solid form. He invited a group of Somalilanders, as well as non Somalilander, to put down their thoughts in a book in a manner that all conerned parties could share. I have contributed a chapter to the second volume of that book. The first volume of the book will be published on May 18, 2011 to coincide with the celebration for Somaliland independence, and in this short article, I bring to you some of the highlights of my thoughts in this matter.

In this 20th anniversary of its independence Somaliland has no choice but to contend with some poignant geopolitical realities. The commonest descriptor that follows its name remains to be the "Self-declared Republic"; the nation has gained no open endorsement and no international reward for 20 years of independent, peaceful existence in a thriving and stable democracy in a corner of the world with high prevalence of strong men, misery and misgovernment. The nation's democratic and secular dispensation remains to be the ultimate target of an Al Shabaab movement that is perpetually gaining strength despite the constant predictions of its imminent defeat and demise. And Somaliland finds itself battling Somali pirates in its shores, unruly tribesmen in its hinterland and vengeful scheming Diaspora based tribal aficionados in the virtual world of web pages and blogospheres (read the nonsensical Awdal Virtual State of Somalia).

Meanwhile the Somali problem has become the epitome of a new version of Murphy's Law. "In the Case of Somalia whenever you think it cannot get any worse, it invariably will". And to sour the mood further Somaliland is increasingly becoming the unintended victim of the fatal side effects that arise from the regional and international efforts of managing and containing the Somali problem. The nation may be running out of time, it is likely to become the victim of the good intensions of its neighbours gone badly or it may find its demise in the hands of the benign neglect of its friends elsewhere. Surviving containment is in the books for Somaliland but the nation has to start thinking in new and innovative ways to overcome the challenges of the radically different and emerging problem of Containment.

Containment: the practice

Containment has become the emergent international response to the chaos in Somalia. It is based on the logical conclusion that the world is neither willing nor capable of solving the Somali problem and that the Somali people have run out of ideas and steam in finding a solution to the crisis that has decimated their population. Yet the twin problems of Somali Piracy and Somali Al Shabaab movement have become too big to be ignored by the international community for they pose significant risk to the life, liberty and pursuit of free commerce in the region and internationally. And so things have just fallen into place and containment has become the accepted practice, the default position so as to limit the bitter fruits of Somali chaos to Somalis only. It is seems as if the same conclusion has been reached in many different capitals of the world simultaneously. When all is said and done the idea of "containment of the Somali problem" provides the best explanatory fit of all or almost all of the recent developments in Somali political, religious and military circumstances. It has successfully dwarfed all attempts at reaching a rational solution or even managing the Somali Crisis. As the Somali proverb says "Biyo Meel Godan Bay isku tagaan" (water collects at the lowest point.) Containment became the trough where water collects.

Containment includes many national, regional and international initiatives that have been gradually gathering pace over the last few years. Many of these steps are mundane and preventative steps like the intense attention and search every Somali triggers at every international port of entry and departure.

In Somalia itself containment crystallized into a subdivision of labour among the active participants in the Somali crisis. The containment of Al Shabaab is subcontracted to regional organizations, and local powers (AU, Ethiopia, Kenya and Uganda, Rwanda and Djibouti). They are the countries that have been willing to put boots on the ground and lives on the line. The containment of Somali Piracy in the high seas and on the ground has become the domain of those with floating flotillas of muscle and manpower, those with experience in the world of espionage, subterfuge and cloak and dagger, and finally those with deep pockets and vested interest that impels them to provide the funding necessary for the introduction of Private Military Companies (PMC) into the action. PMCs for those who don't know is the gentler name for what has been previously called the dogs of war and mercenary forces. Saracen International (which may or may not have ended its involvement in Somali problems) is but just one example among those.

Containment of Al Shabaab

The war in South Somalia today is best explained as the regional attempt of preventing the Al-Qaida affiliated Al Shabaab movement of Somalia from breaking out into a formidable regional force that can threaten its neighbours and the world beyond.

AMISOM with its insufficient numbers and anaemic funding was never really in any position to defeat Al Shabaab or to dislodge the group's hold on Somalia although, this was always and continues to remain its public mask. Never the less AMISOM has succeeded in its real task of denying Al Shabaab the glory and psychological boost of taking over the Somali capital while effectively maintaining the fiction of the existence of a Somali Government.

Ethiopia and more recently Kenya has taken on the role of containing Al Shabaab from the periphery with varying degrees of Success. These neighbouring countries, who were at one time victims of the Somali wars in search of Great Somalia and who may still find themselves in a similar situation in the future have taken on with gusto and dedication to the task of containing Al Shabaab to the regions it now holds in South Somalia.

Ethiopia and to lesser extent Kenya employ Somali tribal militia that they train, arm, pay and fully control for this purpose. They surround Al Shabaab with these tribal militias from the north, west and south and the Indian Ocean completes the circle on the east. Tribal militias are volunteer gangsters whose first loyalty is to the ancestral God of vengeance and honour. The Containment militia however are beholden to a secondary master (Ethiopia or Kenya) for their survival. It is in the nature of tribal militia to fight anyone, Al Shabaab or any other "enemy", provided that they are given a hand against their real enemies that happens to be the neighbouring Somali tribe. That is the nature of the tribal beast. Ethiopia and Kenya understand it well and they have succeeded to put these basal instincts of the Somali tribe to their own good use.

These tribal militias carry different names in various parts of the country. They started life as the militia of Warlords. Sometimes they "elect a president" (usually a Diaspora Somali) and take on the identity of an "xxx state of Somalia". The xxx stands for whatever name the tribe or sub tribe chooses as an acceptable alternate to its name (Galmug State of Somalia, Maakhir State of Somalia Azania State of Somalia, Ximan iyo Xeeb etc). At other times they throw on religious garments and become god's warriors of "Ahlu Sunna Wal Jamma". In the lofty conferences in Nairobi and other high places these tribal militias undergo an ideological abstraction and bureaucratic nomenclature, ending up being referred to as "building blocks", "4.5", "Federal Constitution". It is exceedingly important to deconstruct this terminology for it adds to the confusion of the Somali problem. Here is the essential description of a tribal militia: Its members all belong to the same tribe. Its leader is from the same tribe. It works out of the traditional tribal homeland. Its internal reason for existence is to defend itself from the neighbouring Somali tribe. It can take any name and fight for any "cause" determined by any sponsor that is willing to arm it and assist it in its primary mission.

With these innovations and initiatives AMISOM, Ethiopia and Kenya has so far succeeded to contain Somalia's Al Shabaab Movement to regions it occupies in South Somalia.

Containment: the collateral Damage

Containment is neither as passive nor as peaceful as it sounds. It is an active process of war. It is a low grade chronic warfare that exacts a nagging ever present pain. Containment is a war in which the side that is on the offensive deliberately avoids killer blows and inflicts only small wounds that maim the victim. The intention is to force the victim to die of slow bleeding, starvation and shock. Containment is how the mighty soviet empire was made to collapse under its own weight. To see the modern effect of a war of containment on the body of a nation look no further than Mogadishu, no further than the hundreds of villages that witness the process of containment on a daily basis all over south Somalia. Where are the people of these ghost cities and towns? Why are the morgues full all the time when the streets are so empty, so deserted and so destroyed? The death of Somalis through constant daily bombardment, shelling, displacement and outright murder of large numbers in the active phases of containment in this unfortunate society has become the norm, a common factor that is simply driven out of the equation.

The invisible wounds exacted by Containment run deeper and further into the culture and psyche of the Somali people. The tribal militias of containment (Tribal Homelands, AKA Federal Constitution. AKA Ahlusuna Wal Jama, AKA 4.5, AKA XXX State of Somalia) create a Somali society that is permanently at war with itself. Tribal forces are incapable of living within a state, any state. Wherever you find an armed organized tribal militia you will also find a complete or near complete absence of the state. The two are mutually exclusive. The invisible wound of containment will be the permanent death of a Somali State. In other words under containment Somalia can exist only in the form of a large number of heavily armed tribes, each at war with all of its neighbours and each dependent on Ethiopia or Kenya for its continued existence. The road to hell is paved with good intentions.

Somaliland has become the unintended victim of containment as well. The creation of so many tribal militias, the ready availability of funding from TFG and from international and regional sources interested more in the defeat of Al Shabaab and much less in supporting the independence and stability and democracy of Somaliland has created a tribal storm in the heart of Somaliland. The dangling of a Federal Constitution, which essentially promises each Somali tribe its own state if it is able to establish its credentials by arming itself and fighting against the neighbouring tribe, has created most immediate and toxic environment for Somaliland. Already tribal wars about demarcation of tribal territories have started in eastern part of Somaliland and already tribal hot heads in the Diaspora has started to agitate for war in Awdal State of Somalia in western regions of Somaliland. Furthermore the arrival of mercenaries (Sercen International) in the Puntland State for the dual purposes of strengthening defences against Al Shabaab and going after the pirate lairs on land has destabilized the delicate balance of guns and bullets in the region and has been an essential element for fanning the flames of tribal wars in Somaliland.

Containment has been effective in minimizing the risk from Al Shabaab towards regional and international participants in the Somali conflict. It is has become the death knoll for Somali society and imminent risk to the existence and prosperity of Somaliland.

The Rabi Prophesy

Containment and TFG hoax has allowed neighbouring countries with dubious aims to impose their own designs on Somalia. This tribal sentiment which happens to be the natural inclination of the Somali is fed, armed and inflamed under the direct supervision of Ethiopia and Kenya, two nations that have a vested interest in Somali affairs that may not coincide with that of the Somali people to put it politely.

Ethiopia and Kenya can breathe better now with the concept of Great Somalia dead and its religious reincarnation in the form of Al Shabaab successfully contained. Kenya can now impark in building a democratic society that includes Kenyans of Somali ethnic background. Ethiopia can concentrate on building its infrastructure of roads and dams and electricity as it blissfully waits for its own Tahriir Square moment again with Ethiopians of ethnic Somali origin fully on board. Somaliland agrees with these developments. It wishes for a peaceful co-existence with all of its neighbours. With its own reclamation of its independence on May 18, 1991 Somaliland repudiated completely the concept of Great Somalia. It removed the symbol of Great Somalia, the five pointed star, from its flag and from its other logos. Somaliland realizes that the concept of Great Somalia with its ethnocentric and fascistic flavour has caused immeasurable misery for all Somalis and for all of its neighbours. The central justification of Somaliland's existence is based on the sanctity of the colonial border on the day of its independence in June 26, 1960.

The role Kenya and Ethiopia are currently playing in Somali affairs however goes way beyond the re-affirmation of the colonial border with Somalia. It appears that the hyena has been selected to guard the sheep. And the hyena is being true to its nature. Meles Zenawi now enjoys the honorary status of Grand Reconciliator of Somalia's warring tribes who have developed an intensity of hate for one another that is many times more passionate than their hate for Ethiopia's "occupation of Somali territory of Ogaden, Hawd and Reserve area." Meles may even be in the blessed state of entertaining the now more realistic thought of ending the land locked status of his nation once and for all.

The more a Somali tribe comes to regard the neighbouring tribes with hostility and fear, the more it sees Ethiopia as its trusted friend and protector and the more the tribe finds irresistible the concept of access to a market of 80 million of Ethiopian customers who may be even ready to help them build a seaport in their part of Somalia and a tarmac road for the tribe that connects them to the heart of the beast. These proposed radial Somali-Ethiopian roads could be expected to have the secondary effect of disconnecting each Somali tribe from those on either side of it, as the tribe's social and economic life integrates more organically with that of Ethiopia.

Somaliland which harbours suspicions against Puntland is ready to share the port of Barbara with Meles. Puntland who is engaged in a dispute with Somaliland on one side and who is suspicious of the motives of the Hawiye to the south is ready to share the port of Bosaso and any other ports that can be developed in the region with Meles Zenawi. Galmudug State of Somalia who has similar mutual tribal hostility to the Somali tribes north and south to it plans to build a seaport in Hobyo and then to build a 172 km tarmac road that will connect that port to Meles Zenawi. And this strange affliction of building seaports and radial roads that end up in Ethiopia is going on at the present time in all the shores of Somalia and Somaliland. Meles is adapting, learning and evolving faster than his predecessor on the Ethiopian crown. Why invade Somalia when Somali tribes are begging to belong and to be protected.

In the late nineteen seventies, just before the wars against Siyad Barre started, the great scholar and pan Somali nationalist

Dr. Omer Osman Rabi of Djibouti predicted that Ethiopia will gradually absorb Somali territory and thus achieve its dream of finding access to the sea. Dr. Rabi reached this conclusion by studying the geographical and territorial history of Ethiopia over the last few hundred years. The conclusions of a scholarly analysis that seemed, just twenty years ago, so totally absurd and out of touch with reality appears to be on the verge of becoming real all too soon.

Surviving Containment and Saving the Somali people

There is no doubt that Somaliland has shown an inner resilience, guts and muscle that allowed it to weather many a fatal storm in the past 20 years. It has not only survived but it has prospered and has become a beacon of hope of possibilities that are compatible with life to all Somali people in the horn of Africa. There is no doubt that it will survive this one too aided primarily by its own inner steel and not by any support from any external force.

But Somaliland can and must do more than merely survive this ideological, military and tribal invasion. Somaliland has the promise of bringing something more to the region and to the world at large. It can show the way to an alternative future for Somalis in the horn of Africa and for Ethiopians, Kenyans, and to Djiboutians. A Future that is based on peace not war, on citizens not tribes, on well established colonial borders not the shifting sands of border disputes, primitive tribes with revenge and murder on their minds; future that can allow Ethiopians, Djiboutians, Kenyans and Somalis to prosper together under the stability offered by the sanctity of colonial borders; a future that precludes invasions of neighbouring countries and the building a future of injustice, cruelty, hostility, oppression and subsequent liberations for future generations.

In this regard it is important to realize that what is unique about Somaliland is not that it lacks the destructive power of primitive tribal urges and tribal bloodletting. It has plenty of these. What is unique about Somaliland is that it has stumbled upon a democratic model of governance that can give space to the rise of the concept of a Somaliland citizenship and that opens up for the Somalilander a wider horizon of moral, economic and political action that goes way beyond the narrow confines of tribal identity, tribal wars and tribal revenge. This model of equal citizenship, of one man one vote has given the republican nomad a means of co-existing with other tribes without resorting to the spear and the club as the only arbiter. Somaliland has guarded this uniqueness of its modern existence with all that is at its disposal. Its first line of defence has been to refuse to participate in all Somali reconciliation conferences precisely because every one of these invitations were delivered on the one condition that Somaliland abandon that which is unique about it and that is central to its peace and prosperity (the concept of democratic dispensation, statehood, citizenship, acceptance of colonial borders and the unequivocal and open rejection of Great Somalia.) The open invitations, the behind the scene conspiracies and the secret offers all demanded that Somaliland join its brothers in Somalia on the basis of its tribal subdivision (as Dhulbahante, Gadabuursi, Isaak Issa, Muse Dhariyo, Warsangale and other tribes of Somaliland) and not as a unitary state. Somalilanders knew that the invitation was the Somali tribal offer of "ninkii rooni reerka ha u hadho" (let us fight it out and let the strongest remain standing) and Somaliland rightfully and appropriately rejected every one of these invitations.

And now the time is ripe for a counter offer. Listed below are the necessary elements for the reconstruction of Somali society. Somaliland can succeed in these tasks even though they appear to impossible at first examination. Somaliland must show the willingness to dedicate itself to this course of action until success is achieved. But there is one caveat. Somaliland can only carry such a heavy responsibility if regional and international forces help it achieve these goals and recognize Somaliland as a separate and independent state. In all other circumstance Somaliland should continue to insist on its statehood and independence however long its international recognition takes and however hard the road becomes for the alternative of melting into the Somali problem poses a much more ruthless futue for its population.

The Five Essentials of Reconstruction of Somali Society

1. The military defeat and disarming of all tribal forces, an armed tribe is not compatible with statehood and peace. There can be no compromises here.
2. The military defeat and disarming of all religious groups in a manner that allows space for Salafi, sophism and other versions of Islam to co-exist in peace in a democratic environment.
3. The defeat of piracy at its lairs on land
4. The Resurrection of Somalia in which governance is based on citizenship, not tribal affiliation and land ownership is legally mandated not tribally determined.
5. Open and unequivocal rejection of the concept of Great Somalia and acceptance of the sanctity of colonial borders.

Bringing about such changes to the Somali problem will require both the club and the carrot. It will require many, many dedicated boots on the ground and many more lives on the line. It will require Somalis negotiating with Somalis about the future of Somalis in their own country. Somaliland must start to canvas these thoughts with other Somalis, build the necessary coalitions that could bring it about, avoid the simplistic hair brained "solutions, constitutions, projects, conspiracies and scholarly theses" that are divorced completely from the reality on the ground and the hard work necessary for building a society from the ground up in the field and not in a fancy conference rooms in other countries. Somaliland must allow the means and methodology necessary to complete the task to arise from Somali minds on Somali soil uncontaminated by money, corruption and adverse regional interests. Such consideration must prove themselves real in the harsh hot light of the day in Somalia and on its hard dry grounds where Somalis live, sweat, kill each other and die.

No other nation could be more appropriate, could have deeper commitment, and could be better equipped to deal with the Somali Crisis than Somaliland. No other nation could have a better understanding of the Somali Crisis. No other nation has more profound and fateful vested interest to see the success and rebirth of Somalia. In this initiative Somaliland will be driven by kinship, by self interest and by economic and military necessarily.

... and finally can the world listen to the pleas of Somaliland finally.

CHAPTER 4

Discourse and Intervention in Somaliland: Tensions and successes in the transition from deliberation to representation

Michael Walls, UCL, Steve Kibble, Progressio[38]

Introduction

During his November 2010 visit to the UK, the newly-elected (fourth) President of Somaliland, Ahmed Mohamed Mohamoud 'Silanyo', leader of one of the former opposition parties, Kulmiye, was questioned by many inside and outside the diaspora about his vision for the development of his country, his plans for further democratisation and for gaining recognition as an independent sovereign state. His decisive election victory in June 2010 was declared free and fair by international and domestic observers and the subsequent peaceful handover of power set an important benchmark in what is an increasingly impressive political record in which discursive democratic custom is being gradually melded with the representative institutions of the nation-state. Hopes were high not just that the new government would effect a change from the securocratic and non-transparent practices of former President Riyale, but for a change in the nature of the state towards a more interventionist and pro-poor model.

Many African states struggle to reconcile traditional social institutions with the precepts of nation-state democracy within previously colonial borders. By contrast, it is commonly asserted that the promotion of a human rights culture and of relatively equitable development, requires not only a vibrant civil society but also a strong state capable of implementing policy, listening and responding to grassroots voices and balancing competing pressures.

---

[38] Joint coordinators of the 26 June 2010 Somaliland presidential international election observers.

In Africa the contrasting reality is too often one in which states have inherited colonially-inspired, 'non-rational' borders bearing little relation to pre-colonial power and kinship structures. Such states have attempted to compensate for underdevelopment, overwhelming reliance on unprocessed primary commodities and the lack of a shared tradition of nationhood or legitimacy by heavy centralisation of political power. Numerous leaders have used political power to gain personal economic advantage at the expense of their opponents, or to further narrow kinship interests in a 'winner takes all' struggle for dominance. Consequently, commitment to basic human rights and tolerance of diversity tends to be severely compromised, fostering instead polarised resistance and violent conflict. In many instances, these processes have become institutionalised over some five decades of post-colonial political evolution, entrenching elite-based power struggles that have come to typify the approaches of ruling parties and rebels alike. Even where transfers of power do take place, they exemplify a see-saw pattern in which the polarised nature of politics is further entrenched as one elite simply swaps the spoils of power with another.

In many cases, this can be further analysed as the result of colonial *exploitation* and the consequent and inevitable *corruption* of kinship relations which predated the colonial era and were understood by foreign powers only insofar as they could be used to maintain their external hegemony. The corruption of those institutions became particularly important when the initial mobilisation for the nationalist project faltered. Post-colonial political legitimacy then had to be purchased from key constituencies, kinship networks had to be assuaged and the acquiescence of other groups assured by force. The resources of the state became a means to maintain a hold on power through patrimonialism and clientelism. Given the resulting lack of internal legitimacy, external sources of patronage such as aid and cheap loans became vital. The Cold War saw the opposing powers sustain a large number of dictatorial polities as pawns in a larger game. The Somali Horn of Africa has seen all of these patterns through colonial and post-colonial periods. Indeed, during the Cold War era, Somalia saw some of the highest levels of per capita foreign aid in the world, alternately provided by both Soviet and US sources. It was no coincidence that the government in Somalia, amongst numerous similarly authoritarian regimes, collapsed as soon as that support dried up.

It is often assumed that these post-colonial patterns of state consolidation, coupled with the subsequent dual processes of structural adjustment and globalisation fundamentally disabled the African state. In fact, though, the picture is far more complex than this. Rather than simply succumbing to these forces, states and peoples have in some instances proven an ability to *adapt* to them in a variety of survivalist ways. The problem persists, and even such adaptive patterns are unlikely to be *developmental* in the sense that they could devise or support intentional programmes aimed at bringing significant benefit to most of a given population.

In many instances, people have responded to the situation with a 'flight from the state' into clientelism, clannism or 'tribalism'. State agents themselves have taken part in this process. In what Jean-François Bayart called the 'rhizome' state (Bayart et al., 1999) these agents, along with others, engage in smuggling, tax evasion, drug trafficking, personal control of state resources and other activities that undermine the legitimacy and authority of the state. For instance, Zimbabwe's chaotic - if not completely unsuccessful (Scoones et al., 2010) - land resettlement has had much this effect by maintaining power through degradation of the state, producing a precarious balance between repression and disintegration.

Although African civil society has been important in the unsteady and highly reversible movement towards democratisation, it is a complex phenomenon incorporating both democratic and anti-democratic forces. Civil society requires a form of social contract with the state, and cannot easily strengthen itself when the state is illegitimate. Indeed, illegitimate states tend to be actively intolerant of strong civil societies as they tend to highlight the very reasons for that illegitimacy. Instead, the gap in security and social provision is filled either by external forces, or by private security companies (mercenaries) or warlords. Even in societies where the state has collapsed, including Somalia, markets and trade continue, and indeed flourish, in situations in which state controls supported by public taxation are absent.

None of this is particularly helpful to the mass of the people. They see little potential for a progressive, human rights-oriented developmental state, working to enable them to improve their economic situation. The lack of a functional state makes it more difficult to mobilise resources in the face of catastrophes, with serial droughts in the Somali areas representing just such a case. Similarly, for the majority of people, a non-functional and non-legitimate state serves the wider interests of its citizens poorly in negotiations over resource exploitation, trade and so on. The prognosis for a shift in these destructive and self-perpetuating cycles perhaps supports a less optimistic reading than is often hoped. Recent developments seem to suggest that democratisation movements in Africa are showing themselves to be shallower and shorter-lived than hoped for. The same elites have continued to swap power under the same or slightly wider political and socio-economic arrangements; a situation evidenced in amongst other locations, Kenya and Zimbabwe.

The Somali territories, 'polarities' and external actors

It is against this background that we examine the chances for development and the entrenchment of human rights in the unrecognised state of Somaliland. If indeed, apparent recent progress in improving state legitimacy and broad political participation on the African continent is, on occasion, more chimerical than real, then the apparent successes in the Somaliland case may well offer valuable lessons. However, it is clear that Somaliland itself has seen a process that is particular to the area and its occupants, meaning that such lessons are likely to fall far short of providing a 'model for Somali governance' with wider applicability. Somaliland itself faces significant challenges in a process of transition to representative democracy that inevitably requires difficult social adjustment and will consequently remain fragile for some time to come. Any attempt to draw what lessons might be available requires an acknowledgement of the specificities involved and a clear-sighted review of both challenges and achievements.

A starting point for such an analysis might draw on a number of significant paradoxes pertaining to Somali experiences. Many see the Somali areas in the Horn of Africa as archetypes of state collapse, insurgent activity and conflict between 'traditional', external and Islamist elements. Said Samatar's observation that Somalis are part of a "... a society addicted to congenital egalitarian anarchy" (Said S. Samatar, 2003: 29) would seem to support this view that Somalis are essentially incapable of organising themselves into a centralised system of state. Conversely, Somaliland's sustained period of relative peace, coupled with meaningful and reasonably free elections stands clearly in opposition to this characterisation.

A more nuanced analysis notes the wide regional differences and particularly the successes of Puntland and Somaliland in securing greater stability than is present in the south. At its most optimistic, this alternate perspective sees Somaliland as an example of successful, indigenous state-building against the chronic failure of externally-sponsored initiatives in the south. Indeed proponents of this perspective have suggested that Somaliland could serve as a model for Somalia, with suggestions that Hargeisa be designated the political capital of Somalia while Mogadishu remains divided. For some, the Somaliland experience proves that Somalis will succeed in state-building if (and only if) they are 'left alone' to do so. From this perspective, serial southern failure is laid squarely at the door of an 'international community' whose bungling has exacerbated and perpetuated conflict. In the view of the authors, these proposals are as dependent on a polarised caricature of complex issues as is the case with those who view Somali society as incapable of political organisation. In a globalising international economy, a people whose traditions are strongly anchored in regional and international trade can hardly be 'left alone' in any meaningful sense. The concept of a nation state is itself an external construct, but one with which Somalis must find some accommodation in the long term if Somali society is to thrive in a manner that promotes a general ability to address issues such as climate change-exacerbated environmental fragility.

Both the paradoxes outlined are based on easily packaged polarities, and additional paradoxes become apparent when the basic tenets of each are unpicked. Some view the southern Somali situation as a struggle between the monolithic forces of religion, tradition and an ill-advised 'international community'. The fundamentalist Islamist militia of al-Shabaab is contrasted with the mercenary forces of warlords and those of the internationally supported Transitional Federal Government (TFG). Following a similar logic, state consolidation in Somaliland, and to a lesser extent Puntland, is contrasted with failure in the south, with little or no effort to understand the successes that have been achieved outside Puntland and Somaliland or the ongoing challenges that face those two.

These polarities both fail to provide a basis for an understanding of the potentials for legitimate Somali state formation, and misrepresent the evidence on ways in which 'outsiders' in the Somali context might help or hinder those processes. In so doing, they obscure what are almost certainly more helpful observations than are supported by the caricatures themselves.

In an effort to provide more useful depth to the discussion, this paper now turns its attention to the specifics of the political environment in Somaliland. In the first instance, we must provide some background, looking slightly further back, before focusing on the run-up to the presidential elections that took place in June 2010, the elections themselves and the early period of the government that took power as a result of those elections.

Background to Somaliland

The Republic of Somaliland unilaterally declared independence from Somalia in 1991, after a civil war had caused the collapse of the dictatorial Siyaad Barre regime. In doing so, they were announcing the restoration of the independence they enjoyed for several days in 1960, and based on colonial borders. This represented an end to the territory's allegiance to a greater Somalia. While the southern areas of Somalia entered a sustained period of endemic conflict, interspersed with unsuccessful periodic, peace conferences, the people and clans of Somaliland embarked on a home-grown process of reconciliation and state-building, largely escaping the pressure of outside-brokered and lavishly-funded interventions aimed at establishing a government for the whole of the erstwhile Republic of Somalia.

In the late 1990s, Somaliland's political leadership declared a commitment to representative democracy, with local elections in 2002, a presidential election in 2003, and parliamentary elections in 2005 all contributing to that process. This process of representative democratisation has, unsurprisingly, faced numerous problems and obstacles, including two periods marked by a return to conflict, albeit on a limited basis. In the period immediately following the 1991 declaration of renewed sovereignty, the SNM, the very insurgent movement that had played a key role in bringing down the Siyaad Barre regime, imploded. Distrust between erstwhile allies flared into violence in Burao, then turned to outright war in Berbera in a dispute over control of the port facilities.

That conflict resulted in a significant setback for the government, and the President allowed a council of elders to assume a mediatory role. Notably, the core of that council was provided by two clans who had tended to side against the SNM during the insurgency: the Gadabuursi and the Dhulbahante. In effect elders from those two groups mediated as 'interested outsiders', ultimately convening a major national conference in the western town of Borama (Walls, 2009). That conference saw a peaceful transfer of power from the SNM military administration to a civilian president.

The second recurrence of conflict bore a significant similarity to the Berbera one. It too was fuelled in part by a contest between government and clan for control of a key piece of infrastructure; in this case, Hargeisa airport. That conflict dragged on for several years, starting shortly after the Borama conference and not finding complete resolution until another major clan conference in 1997 in Hargeisa.

The Hargeisa conference was hosted by the government, and so cannot be seen as resting on the intervention of outsiders. In fact, it has long been criticised for that reason, described by many as 'politicised'. Nevertheless, that conference succeeded in finding the consensus on which a period of peace extending to the present time was built.

The pattern throughout these first years of Somaliland's self-declared independence is notable for the pragmatism of those involved, as well as the cycle of crisis and resolution. That is a cycle which was well in evidence in the build up to the successful 2010 election, and closer review is instructive in laying a foundation for answers to some of the questions raised previously.

From Crisis to Election: Discourse and intervention

In general terms, the crisis was precipitated by the incumbent government's attempts to cling to power after 2008 without a legitimate political mandate. The government failed to prepare for elections in a timely fashion, and engaged in blatant politicking aimed at extending the president's term through questionably constitutional avenues. The opposition on several occasions added to the crisis by playing their own political games, and seeming to push the country towards a standoff that held many of the attributes of the factionalised politics that have characterised the politics of the transitional government in the south.

Eventually, though, a return to the discursive traditions of the post-1991 period, assisted by opportune external engagement, enabled a notably successful election.

Resolution of the stand-off came about through a late 2009 agreement on a six-point memorandum. This defused the situation described earlier, which had by then led to violent protest and the deaths of demonstrators. Here the donor group fulfilled a function outlined in brief some months before (ISG, 2009). They simultaneously maintained a strong position on a number of prerequisites for their renewed support for elections while also engaging in supportive diplomacy with UK representatives in particular working through the Ethiopian Deputy Foreign Minister. Using this combination of muscular and supportive diplomacy, these external representatives were able to draft a 'non-paper'[39] which subsequently reappeared as the draft for a six-point memorandum signed by the key Somaliland stakeholders (Kibble and Walls, 2009; Walls, 2009).

It is notable that successful interventions such as this tend to be smaller in scale and built actively on local initiatives. In each case, external funding did not disproportionately dominate, and outsiders did not establish frameworks and deadlines beyond the immediate release of funds. These critical decisions were made by local actors who then had to face their own constituents. External actors did not escape criticism by any means; they were seen as active participants in a contentious process and therefore, for many observers, complicit in bad decisions and deserving of condemnation. However, by not dominating proceedings as hosts, primary funders, or the deliverers of state-building frameworks, outsiders were able to adjust their positions as events unfolded, ultimately remaining engaged.

In short, despite increasingly autocratic and anti-democratic government moves up until September 2009, socio-political norms that emphasised the importance of negotiation and compromise averted what was shaping up to be a serious crisis. In marked contrast to efforts in southern Somali areas, cautious

---

[39] The 'non-paper' is a useful EU concept that does not commit authors or readers to a course of action and is not intended to be read as a policy intervention, but rather as a contribution to debate. However, non-papers do have a habit of becoming part of the policy-making process in spite of those intentions.

and fully engaged external interventions were successful in supporting that process. We have also argued elsewhere (Walls and Kibble, 2010) that outsiders in Somaliland have been able to move things forward on a number of occasions by building on local initiatives, resources and traditions. External intervention has, on occasion, achieved significant success in breaking through roadblocks where local negotiations have stalled. Somali custom explicitly creates space in which outsiders may assume constructive roles, with such activities periodically playing a decisive part in resolving significant difficulties.

Nevertheless, it is notable that, as successful as they have been, this combination of indigenous negotiation and occasional and engaged external involvement remains incomplete. Despite mythologies to the contrary, the transition continues to rely on external inputs from both non-Somali and diasporic agents.

Conversely, it is hard to argue that external interventions in the south have served as anything other than a cumulatively malign influence over the long term. Our point is simply that, while external interventions have been spectacularly unsuccessful in some instances, a measured reading of processes to date nevertheless undermines the oft-stated conclusion that 'Somalis will succeed if only they are left to themselves'. There is in fact real and substantial evidence that external engagement plays an extensive, varied and sometimes pivotally important role in the Somali context.

The argument that 'outsiders' should withdraw altogether from engagement springs from sources both Somali and non-Somali, and is employed in a variety of instances. We argue in contradiction that active and informed engagement from external agents is essential if past advances are to be built upon. Indeed, it is a mistake to presume that 'outsiders' constitute a single group or that the term should be used only when considering non-Somali agents. The large and active diaspora is itself a diverse set of external groups, while groups or individuals who sit outside a given dispute have long played an essential role in peace-making within Somali society. Somaliland's contemporary history provides useful illustration of these processes, as well as giving some indication of ways in which non-Somalis can also play a positive role.

Much of that process, including the recent retreat from crisis, has been enabled by an overwhelming public desire to avoid a return to conflict and an accompanying urge to win international recognition (although yoking the two has also proved problematic). The nascent state remains weak and poorly-funded, but has paradoxically enjoyed a degree of legitimacy exceeding that of many African and other governments. However, until the recent elections, the institutionalisation of a system that combines elements of traditional 'pastoral' male democracy in the context of the Westphalian and Weberian nation-state seemed to be starting to unravel. In its place a personalised 'securocratic' approach was gaining the upper hand, with a concomitant fear of debate and criticism. This intolerance of dissent is at odds with Somali tradition more generally and can be seen as a legacy of the Siyaad Barre regime. However, it remains to be seen how deeply embedded it is as we move into the era of a new government and a promised more open, transparent society rethinking its engagement with outsiders as well as internal policy.

It is worth noting also that a potentially far more destructive external presence was also very evident prior to the election. Indeed, the poll went ahead despite serious concerns over security, the relevance of which were graphically illustrated by a shootout between political Islamists and police in Somaliland's second city of Burao in early June. That action appeared to have dismantled a well-planned anti-Somaliland operation. Just before election day, the Islamist organisation al-Shabaab based in (south central) Somalia warned Somalilanders against voting – 'advice' Somalilanders ignored by turning out in large numbers. Security considerations had led some international organisations to adopt a 'hibernation' mode or to send staff out of the country. The bombings in Kampala a month later illustrated the fragility of the security situation, while also underlining the fact that, increasingly, Somali insecurity extends beyond Somali borders.

Political Islamism represents yet another form of externality: the fundamentalism of al-Shabaab owes far more to an imported Salafist tradition than it does to the more mystical Sufism most favoured in Somali society to date.

New Government: Early performance and policy possibilities

The same internal and external forces continue to play vital roles in Somaliland. The presence of many diaspora members in the cabinet underlines the importance of links with a world outside the immediate confines of the Somali Horn. International attitudes to Somaliland, too, are changing.

Many now look to the new government for the implementation of new approaches to overcoming the previous stasis in the arenas of justice, further democratisation and development. There are a number of questions that will determine fundamentally the ways in which traditional institutions interact with the norms of nation-state democracy. Clan will continue to play a significant yet dynamic role in the political realm, while external actors, from private, public and non-governmental sectors, must also expand their involvement.

On the first day of the new regime, the government delivered on a pledge to abolish the unpopular security committees. Originally established to address urgent issues of security in the wake of the civil war, these committees had been permitted to imprison without trial and they lay outside any due judicial process. A new National Security Board has been established instead, with a mandate that embraces the security of the country, defence of its borders and the fight against terrorism.

There has as yet been no effect on other parts of the judicial system from this policy change. The judiciary remains ineffective and subject to executive pressure arising from its lack of independence. It is also alleged to be corrupt and non-professional with untrained clerks acting as judges. A seasoned observer described the system as 'a hell of a mess which will take a lot of cleaning up. It's still based largely on judicial practice under Siyaad Barre – i.e. who has the most money wins'.

The position of women has been another key element in the fight to further and deepen democratisation and Kulmiye has, as well as its clan base, majority support among women, youth, civil society and diaspora. We spoke to key activists on the subject, and they cautiously welcomed the increase in female cabinet ministers from 5% to 20% but pointed out this still only means two ministers and an assistant minister. (We do note however that the cabinet has shrunk in size.) There is also a woman commissioner on the Human Rights Commission. The new (female) Minister for Labour and Social Affairs is, unlike her predecessor, open to dialogue with civil society. Women's groups welcomed these developments, with the umbrella network Nagaad promptly submitting an advisory paper on gender issues to the government. However, women's groups are looking for much more tangible progress and this still appears largely distant. There is, for example, little noticeable movement on key issues such as proposed 30% quotas for women in parliament.

There has more generally been movement on a much improved relationship with civil society. A new NGO Act defining roles and responsibilities for NGOs as well as giving them legal protection was signed into being while a number of new ministers have civil society backgrounds. These include one of the female cabinet members, Zamzam Abdi, now Minister of Higher Education and formerly Executive Director of the Committee of Concerned Somalis (CCS) and ex-Chair of the human rights network, SHURONET. The new Minister of Planning was himself a founding member of the NGO Somali Relief Association (SOMRA) in the UK in the early 90s, and spent the past few years working with the private sector hawala (money transfer company), Dahabshiil. Early in his new ministerial role, he held his first coordination meeting with the UN and international NGOs and presented new guidelines for aid coordination. In addition, there is the promise of forums for domestic civil society to engage with government and to monitor performance, including input into the budgetary process. However there has been disquiet expressed over this new

NGO law in that it could undermine international humanitarian work according to aid workers and donors. While establishing a legal framework for NGOs, to ensure their activities are in line with the government's development priorities and to improve accountability and transparency is fine in principle, much of the wording of the law appears ambiguous. Foreign agencies working in Somaliland are particularly worried about article 35(3), which states: "International NGOs shall not become implementers for other international NGOs and UN organisations working in the country."

While the aim of encouraging international NGOs and UN agencies to work with local NGOs and businesses on the implementation of projects building domestic capacity is laudable, there are fears that a blanket application of the principle, rather than a case-by-case approach, could drastically reduce overall donor funding. Some programmes being carried out require specific technical expertise that is not easily available in-country.

Another issue is that the Act empowers the government of Somaliland to determine where aid should go. Specifically, t This flouts a fundamental humanitarian principle aid allocation should be decided solely on the basis of need. There also appears to be some ambiguity in the law as to whether this provision appl as development aidities for clarity on more than two dozen of the Act's provisions.

Before the elections, the (then Shadow) Foreign Minister spoke of taking a far more nuanced approach to Somaliland's neighbours, including pursuing reconciliation with Somalia and Puntland, as well as with other Somali groups and neighbours in the Horn in general. This necessarily requires that Somaliland address specific sensitivities on the question of recognition, on which neighbours remain the key.

In a recent talk in London, one of the authors of this editorial floated the concept of 'incremental recognition' in which we suggest that Somaliland leaders engage in confidence-building measures, such as pursuing the possibility of greater engagement with regional bodies such as the IGAD forum

(Intergovernmental Authority on Development). The premise is that this would allow Somaliland themselves to assume a more active and self-directing role in the pursuit of recognition, setting modest incremental objectives that are nevertheless achievable and should one day lead to a situation in which full recognition represents mere acceptance of an ipso facto condition. Such an approach would contrast with past tendencies to emphasise recognition as a one-stop solution requiring a single, substantial policy shift on the part of other nations.

Some months after the election, IGAD extended an invitation to Somaliland to send a representative to an IGAD meeting in Addis Ababa as an observer, so perhaps the engagement with IGAD is indeed deepening.

Since taking office, there has been an unexpectedly positive presidential visit to Djibouti in which President Silanyo was awarded red carpet status as if he were a recognised head of state. The long-closed Somaliland liaison office was also reopened, marking a shift from the rocky relations between Djibouti and the Riyale regime. It may be that this change is linked to the new fibre-optic cable coming into Somaliland via Djibouti. A number of government advisers themselves have links with Djibouti, and there were accusations within Somaliland that the agreement had favoured Djibouti against Somaliland interests.

Having initially viewed the new Somaliland government with suspicion, Ethiopia also hosted a Somaliland delegation led by Mohamed Abdillahi Omar, the new Minister of Foreign Affairs. In so doing they indicated a willingness to work with the new administration. Hargeisa has also seen a visit from the new UN Envoy to Somalia, apparently at the invitation of the Norwegian Refugee Council. Significantly, the Executive Secretary of IGAD, Mahboub Maalim, also visited Sheikh Veterinary School and met with the President, noting that his visit marked a new era in the relationship between IGAD and Somaliland.

However, relations with Puntland have continued to be tense, with the contested sovereignty of areas of Sanaag and Sool complicated by recent accusations from Puntland that Somaliland was harbouring and indeed promoting the 'terrorist' Mohamed Said 'Atom'. Puntland forces had clashed with Atom in the mountainous area of Galgala, and accused Somaliland variously of sending militia to fight alongside him and of sheltering him when he fled. The Somaliland account inevitably differed from this, with senior politicians declaring Atom a terrorist and insisting that the two territories were cooperating over terrorism. These claims were repeated to us when we spoke to the Somaliland President and the Minister of Foreign Affairs in London in November, who suggested that the dispute was essentially between the Puntland administration and local clan groups.

Another disappointing trend has seen a continuation of the tendency of previous administrations to solve disagreements with the media by imprisoning journalists on dubious charges. One of most high profile early instances involved the suspension of the right of the popular Somali cable broadcaster Universal TV to work in Somaliland. The reason given was that Universal had consistently 'treated Somaliland unfairly'. The ban was rescinded, but then renewed when the broadcaster was caught displaying images of the bodies of militia killed outside Somaliland, whileclaiming they were casualties of Somaliland forces. More recently, the Chief Editor of YOOL daily newspaper was threatened by ministers and security personnel for unfavourable coverage. Mahamud Abdi Jama, editor of the daily newspaper 'Waaheen' which belongs to Ahmed Hussein Essa – a long-time politician with good insider knowledge but with a combative past inside Kulmiye – was also arrested for publishing articles which accused the government of nepotism. Mahamud was sentenced to three years in prison and fined. He was subsequently granted a presidential pardon after global pressure on the government and released after spending over a month in prison. He was then awarded the Free Press Africa Award for 2011 at the CNN Multichoice African Jof the Year ceremo

However, this did not stop condemnation from the National Union of Somali Journalists (NUSOJ) over continuing intimidation of journalists. Following the arrest in Berbera on

10 May of a reporter from the Hargeisa-based Haatuf daily newspaper, Ahmed Adan Hirsi (also known as Ahmed Dhere), the NUSOJ was again moved to complain. "It is inconceivable that suddenly, the Somaliland authorities decided to take such repeated and repressive actions against journalists who were only fulfilling their duty to inform the general public about what is happening in their communities," said Omar Faruk Osman, NUSOJ Secretary General. NUSOJ alleges that "the numerous attacks, beatings, fines and legal actions suffered by journalists in Somaliland at the hands of Somaliland public officials, police, CID and judiciary system are in complete violation of the constitution, human rights and freedom of press." They urged the political powers in Somaliland to refrain from pressuring media houses and journalists. "While we call for the immediate release of Ahmed Adan Hirsi, we further insist that Somaliland supports and fosters an independent media environment instead of obstructing it" added Omar Faruk.

Hopes that the new administration would not resort systematically to the measures of the prior regime have begun to fade – even though the new media spokesperson for the government is himself an ex-journalist. Whileso far less guilty of unrandue harassainsa significant need for work on fully institutionalising the freedom of the media, particularly in such areas as making defamation a civil rather than a criminal offence, and in removing the means for local governors to initiatethe extra-legal arrest of journalists.

The Somaliland media must surely be seen as an important component in a transition from discursive to representative politics. It seems self-evident that, for that transition to continue to evolve positively, 'modern' media institutions must play a role in perpetuating discourse. It must be noted that newspapers such as YOOL deliberately strike a strident and controversial position. More mainstream papers are also guilty of biased and under-researched journalism on occasion – although this is hardly the particular prerogative of Somaliland journalists. Whether such positions ultimately undermine or strengthen public discourse remains an open question, but it must be incumbent on both government and the media themselves to seek a constructive role in the process.

There are many both in Somaliland and in the diaspora who feel the administration has failed to display sufficient vision in their actions and leadership. Some charge that Kulmiye did not have a plan for governing, concentrating too hard on winning the election on an anti-government platform and, despite the high expectations of the population, they are now weighed down by the day-to-day job of government. A popular joke asks whether 'change' meant 'change of ministers and staff'. One commentator opined that the President seems to be overwhelmed and that he lacks the stamina for the job, relying instead on others to do the work for him.

It is still too early to tell whether such criticism is well-founded. The first year of the presidency has seen considerable advance as well as areas of disappointment. It is unreasonable to claim, as some have, that it is a sign of weakness that the President has gathered a group of trusted ministers around him. Indeed, it would surely be the height of conceit and a measure of incompetence were a president to attempt to govern without trusted and responsible assistance. However, complaints about a lack of vision and unnecessary levels of negativity perhaps hold more validity. Too many civil servants were fired for what appeared no fault of their own other than (inevitable) ties to the prior administration. In the process, competent as well as less able individuals were lost. Equally, there have been concerning indications that the administration has lacked a consistent agenda, with ministers too willing to embark on action at odds with the positions of other members of the executive. It is possible that the anti-media moves described were a manifestation of this tendency.

Ultimately, criticism is a mark of both discourse and representative democracy. The transition will have passed yet another milestone if that criticism starts to focus more on policy and less on what must certainly in part be kinship-related personal attacks. As noted previously, that is part of a difficult transition, but it is one in which Somaliland have made great strides to date.

Extending our view to the wider geopolitical arena, the 2010 presidential election greatly increased the likelihood that external powers will grant greater legitimacy to the state as donors and powerful international actors seek to reward the country for a significant consolidation of past democratic gains. There is potential for that role to be positive, provided the Somaliland state proves itself capable of negotiating robustly and in the interests of a broad domestic polity. Equally donors should be raising questions as to the proclaimed democratic practices of a democratising (and developmental) state. A discursive dialogue following Somali practice would seem to be indicated, although donor deadlines will make this difficult.

Shortly after the election, there was considerable evidence of donor goodwill. In September, the US Assistant Secretary of State for African Affairs announced a new policy on Somaliland that would see 'aggressive' engagement with the administrations there and in Puntland (Carson, 2010). Such engagement will inevitably be highly focused on an anti-terrorist/political Islamist agenda, so these words are not necessarily reassuring for Somalis in general. For Somaliland specifically, though, they may be more helpful.

As Somaliland attempts to reach out more actively and to establish a more nuanced approach to international and regional players, increasing international acceptance of Somaliland as an autonomous political entity could assist significantly. The US shift is part of a 'dual track' strategy which will see the US continue to support the Mogadishu-based Transitional Federal Government, but which is also meant to result in an increase in direct aid to Somaliland, so the possibility for this and similar adjustments in attitude to result in tangible benefit for Somaliland is real. One year after the election, and nine months after the statement itself, though, there is little concrete evidence of a genuine shift in US action. Perhaps the action will follow in due course.

The UK position too has changed. In that case significant adjustments to DFID's aid allocation plus extended Foreign and Commonwealth Office engagement with the territory were presaged by much more low key public statements. Overall UK aid to the Somali territories is set to increase threefold while Somaliland's share of that larger total also increases. These shifts are likely to have a significant impact on Somaliland, and if managed well could represent another positive external engagement.

The British Ambassador to Ethiopia, a Danish minister, and a team led by the Swedish Ambassador to Kenya all also promised to channel an increased proportion of aid directly to Somaliland and there has been some talk of budget support for the government – perhaps channelled through some sort of trust fund. If implemented, this would mark a significant shift in donor engagement with Somaliland, contributing materially to the process of incremental recognition mentioned above. However, these discussions are yet to result in action.

Finally, Somaliland has a significant opportunity at the present time given the impending expiry of the mandate of the Transitional Federal Government in the south. This is particularly so with the European Union, one of the major financiers of Amisom and the Somali Transitional Federal Government, threatening to cut further support if the current office holders do not relinquish power when their term of office comes to an end in August. The TFG has long represented an explicit obstacle if Somaliland is to extend the depth and breadth of its formal engagement with the international community. Negotiation with donors over their future strategies therefore represents a very real opportunity for Somaliland, along with those amongst the international diplomatic community who would like to see a change in the nature of that engagement, to leverage a further and more substantial enhancement in international acceptance of Somaliland. But a genuine conversation on what each side means by democracy and development will, as we suggest above, be necessary.

Conclusion

The election of a fresh administration in Somaliland promised much and in the first twelve months of their term they have delivered on some of that promise. Early moves to disband security committees and to improve relations with civil society have been welcome (even if problems remain), and significant successes have been achieved in foreign policy. Set against these advances have been continued harassment of media representatives, albeit so far at a lower level than was the practice of the previous government. Similarly, a policy of unnecessary replacement of civil servants provided fuel to those complaining that the administration was too narrowly focused on clan and political appointment.

There is also some merit to the criticism that the government has failed to display a genuinely coherent leadership for the country. Again, this is an area in which the previous administration was signally poor, so setting a low benchmark. It is small comfort therefore that the new government has at least improved on that record.

The administration has commendably attempted to extend the development process to the east of the country. However, set against that effort has been an unfortunate record of so far relatively minor conflict in Sool. That dispute also displays the interplay of discourse and external intervention when the dominance of diasporic actors in both the Somaliland government and their militant eastern protagonist, the SSC[40] is noted.

Above all, though the processes that are described in this chapter, both general and specific, involve an active dialogue between the institutions of customary discourse and those of representative democracy. Indubitably it lies in Somaliland's

---

[40] The SSC initials denote the Somali regions of Sool, Sanaag and Cayn, although the group is primarily active in a small area of Cayn around Buuhoodle and into Sool. The SSC leadership have been outspoken in identifying themselves as diaspora returning 'to fight for their territory', and much of the group's financial support is channeled through clan affiliates from diasporic communities.

interest, and that of her people, to find the accommodations in these areas that will allow the territory to engage actively and constructively with the rest of the world. Somalis have always done just that, and the large diaspora from both northern and southern Somali territories demonstrates the importance, indeed inevitability, of a deepening and consolidating relationship between Somaliland in particular, and the Somali areas in general and a highly complex and interlinked network of internal and external agents.

Many of the discursive institutions that have successfully supported resource-based conflict have also been shown to be adaptable to the exigencies of nation-state politics. However, the transition from one to the other is neither automatic nor easy. Somaliland offers many instructive clues on the kinds of approaches that might be effective – both for domestic and international actors. However, the territory does not suggest a model for state-building.

CHAPTER 5

In memory of Ibrahim Megag Samatar
[Qollad (Hargeysa, Somaliland), 1942(?) - Togane (Tokyo, Japan), 2011]

Jama Musse Jama

I dedicated this book to Ibrahim Megag Samatar for his strong sense of duty, mission and personal sacrifice; for his passion and love for his country. I dedicated to him because he inspired a great deal of my generation, and it is our responsibility to tell the forthcoming generations of Somalilanders that there have been men and women like Ibrahim Megag Samatar who laid down a solid foundation for their nation. This chapter is in honor of this leader, and his writings, included here, reveal his loyalty and true intentions for his country.

The first paragraph want to document a short biography of the late Ibrahim Megag Samatar. The rest of the chapter presents three selected of his recent works. The "Light At the End of the Tunnel: Some Reflections on the Struggle of the Somali National Movement" was written at a time of great uncertainty in Somaliland, in the midst of the fratricidal civil war of the mid 90s but it still struck an optimistic note in regards to Somaliland`s future prospects. "Where I stand" was written in 2009 to reiterate his loyalty to the "Somaliland project" and, according to his daughter Shukri, *"in this article he laid out his visions for Somaliland and his view on topics such as good governance and Islam."* This piece served also as a sort of framework for his later writing and what would eventually become the first chapter of his unfinished book. His son Rage described how he found the third selected article from the notes of the late professor Samatar: *"I came to discover my late Father`s last piece of writing and undoubtedly it was about his beloved Somaliland. A few days after my Father`s passing I was tasked with cleaning out his office at the campus* *of Josai International University in Togane and while packing away my Father's huge collection of books my eye caught a glimpse of a notebook pad sitting on his desk and when I opened it I was so surprised and touched that I broke down in tears. It was the first chapter of a book my Father was writing on Somaliland and the history of the Somali National Movement."*

I am thankful to professors Hussein Adam and Richard Ford, the editors of the volume "Mending Rips in the Sky: Options for Somali Communities in the 21st Century" and their publisher Red Sea Press for the permission to include the article "Light At the End of the Tunnel: Some Reflections on the Struggle of the Somali National Movement". I am also thankful to the members of the late Ibrahim Megag Samatar's family for their help to make sure to record an accurate data for this short biography account. In particularly I thank Shukri I. M. Samatar and Rage I. M. Samatar for sharing me with their essays on their father, and for verifying the correct editions of the unpublished works included here. I thank Mohamed Omer Meigag for giving me the permission to publish some of photographs included in this book, including the picture on the cover.

Short biography

A former Planning Minister for Somali Republic, Ibrahim Megag Samatar was a cabinet member of the Siyad Barre regime for nine years and then Ambassador in West Germany for one year. He served in different periods of time as Minister of Finance and Minister of Industry before he started leading National Planning. He eventually defected and sought asylum in the United States and then joined the Somali National Movement (SNM), the major armed liberation movement against the dictator who fought Siyad Barre regime. For SNM, Ibrahim Megag Samatar became the chairman of their Central Committee. When Somaliland regained its independence, he served as the Chair of the interim National Assembly in Somaliland.

Based on his passport, he was born on February 20th, 1942 but his real birth date was sometime in between 1939 and 1941, a period known also as *Waktigii baandada* (bandit era). His passport indicates that he was born in Hargeysa but actually he was born in Qullad, somewhere in between Awaare and Hargeysa in the Hawd reserved area.

Ibrahim Megag Samatar studied at Yale University and University of California, Riverside. In 1997, after a long and illustrious career in Somali politics, diplomacy, and academia, he moved to Japan where he was been a professor of economics at the Josai International University in Togane, Japan, just outside Tokyo. He lived there until his death when he passed away on January 31st 2011. In Japan, he taught many subjects such as International Politics, International Economics, Economics Theory, Arabic and Islamic Studies at Josai International University in Togane.

Ibrahim Megag Samatar is survived by his wife, Amina Jama Hassan, a son (Rage) and two daughters (Luul and Shugri).

Ibrahim Megag Samatar in a moment of celebration at SOPRI
Somaliland Convention, Washington, 2006

Ibrahim Megag Samater receives in his Embassy office Karl Carstens,
Bundestag President, Secretary of State Federal Foreign Office, Federal
Republic of Germany, Bonn, 1980 (photo from commons.wikimedia.org)

Where I Stand
By Ibrahim Meygag Samater, August 2009

Introduction

My name is Ibrahim Megag Samater. I was a Cabinet member of the Siyad Barre regime for nine years and then his Ambassador in Bonne for one year. In 1981, I defected from his regime and sought asylum in the US. After a few years, I became active in the liberation movement against the dictator, becoming one of the leaders of the Somali National Movement (SNM). Even though my official job was the representative of the movement in North America, more than half of my time was spent in the field among the elders and militants, risking my life several times. My last task in the SNM was as chairman of its Central Committee. My most exhilarating moment in that struggle was in Burao, May 1981, when as chairman of the Central Committee, I had to announce officially the decision of the people of Somaliland to restore their sovereignty.

After the Borama Conference in early 1993, I was elected as a member of the House of Representatives. But, I immediately resigned to pick up the pieces of my life, which I have sacrificed so much during the struggle. Since then, I have been mostly silent on political issues. I feared that my words would be misinterpreted. I had no intention to create any problems for my people. One can only give so much if you are sincere. Now that I have been away for so long and I am not in any competition for a political post, it may be about time for me to speak. In thus speaking, I am not in the business of personal attacks and condemnations. I intend to stick to the higher field of principles and morals. What I want to do here is a statement of principles. It is mainly for the younger generation to whom the future belongs. These are simple words of principle from a retired man. This statement as such, is simply to clarify for citizens of Somaliland where they are going and what their future is to be and where they are to go from here. The future is theirs and the decisions are theirs. All I want to do now is to state in a concise manner what the outlining principles should be as I see them. I am outlining here some major issues of principle of which the wider public should know of every "politician's" position. Without further ado let me list some of these issues of principle.

I-On Somali Unity

This was an issue of great importance for all Somalis everywhere and anywhere during the struggle for independence. The goal was to unite all the Somali territories that have been divided by the colonial masters. As a young high school student, I was one of those who were totally absorbed by that issue. As a student and later as a responsible adult, I fought for that cause. We all know the story now. To unite all Somalis and their territories became impossible in the present state of the international arena – There is no need to go into details. Now, Djoubti is an independent country, the Somalis in Ethiopia and Kenya are trying to get their luck and rights in those countries where they live. We were then left with the union of Somaliland and Somalia alone. Even though Somaliland, before 1960, had more economic trade and other relations with Djoubti and Ethiopia, it opted for unity with Mogadishu for the sake of that larger cause. It was not to be and yet the union between Hargeisa and Mogadishu became sour. The union kicked off without real negotiations and sound legal foundations (this was the fault of the people and leadership of Somaliland). It started with inequality with Somaliland being treated as simply a backyard province rather than a country, which sacrificed its sovereignty for the sake of larger unity. As long as the democratic system was in place people entertained the hope that change for the better was possible. But after the military coup a slow process of recolonizing Somaliland by Somalia began until, in the later years of the regime, it culminated in total suppression, destruction, and attempted genocide. In such conditions, resistance was inevitable. In 1991, the resistance succeeded, the regime disintegrated, Somaliland restored its sovereignty, and Somalia ran into uncontrollable mayhem which is still continuing.

What needs to be done now is :
- Somalilanders should stick to their sovereignty
- Those in Somalia have no choice but to accept that sovereignty

When Somalia reaches that stage the two states should become friendly and work out their relationships in a fraternal manner and after that work on a more rational relationship in the Horn of Africa.

The different governments that succeeded one another in Somaliland were all dedicated to seeking recognition from the international community, as was the general public. In order to forestall this issue, with which we all concur, from becoming a bone of contention between those contending for power, let us make it a collective effort in which the executive, the legislative bodies, the political parties and civil society associations all take their part. This is a process that has already started but it needs to be formalized and structured. This approach led of course by the executive will enable us not only to take initiatives in the countries we consider vital, but also to be present in every international and regional meeting or conference where Somali issues at large are being discussed, without becoming one of the Somalia factions. Up to now our public were suspicious that the leadership may reach an accommodation, which undermines the sovereignty of Somaliland and as such the various governments were prevented from making our voice heard in such forums. The new collective approach should dispense with that suspicion and may even enable us to gain some friends in Somalia for our cause. When and if the opportunity arises we may also be of some help in their reconciliation. This will also speedy up the attainment of our recognition. I believe Somaliland has reached a stage that is beyond fear on this score.

II- On Democracy

Democracy is one of the misunderstood, misinterpreted and misused words in the political vocabulary of the world. Again, these words are not a treatise in political science, so I do not want to go into further analysis. But, in the context of our situation in Somaliland certain points have to be highlighted. The essential content of democracy is that political rule must be based on the consent of the governed – the people. This can take many forms, some better than others. It has been experimented in many ways in many places throughout human history.

We Muslims know democracy. It has been practiced in the early days of Islam. The basic principles are enshrined in the Quran. Those who are sceptical about this matter please read Surat 'Ala-Umran.'

Nevertheless, I do not believe that the present form of democracy through multiparty system and one person-one-vote is evil. It is only one of the forms of democracy that has been performed and practiced by humans. And it is fine if we continue to improve it. Having said that, I do not believe that the multiparty system is a cure for all our ills. It hast to be complemented by our cultural and religious traditions. Otherwise, the parties will become a shell without content. They will become a façade for a new type of dictators who dominate their parties preventing their members and their voters at large to have a real choice.

There is a simple way to avoid that pitfall. Let our democracy be participatory rather than formal. The way to do it is two-fold:
- Let the parties themselves be democratic. There should be registered members at the lowest level who pay their subscriptions. These members should be able to elect their committees and representatives at all level all the way to the top of the leadership. This means that the members of the Party will have a common programme to which they are committed and a leadership, which they trust, rather than nepotism. If this is not done the political parties, which we are imitating from the West will just deteriorate into clan affiliations with all their inherent conflicts.
- The second means is decentralization of the administration. This should not be a formal statement. It must be enshrined

by law and put into practice from the villages, districts and regions. These organs must be able to not only elect their leaders but conduct their own development projects and their administrations. What is left for the Central Government would be co-ordination, planning and keeping the peace of the nation at large.

III-On the Guurti and Clannism

What I have said above in no way negates the importance of clans. They are institutions that have evolved through the ages and enabled us to survive. Unless the function clanism performs is replaced by other institutions it is not going away. But, we know it is a double-edged sword. Depending on how it is handled by the leaders of the time, whether they are elders or politicians, clanism can be a good tool for peace, reconciliation and progress. Handled wrongly it is a powerful tool for fratricide and conflict. Just look at what is happening in Somalia (the former South). The question is what to do with this double-edged sword in our cultural tradition. It has been the genius of the SNM struggle to find a way out. Making the Guurti, representing traditional leadership, a constitutional political body, rather than peripheral individuals which the then authorities can use them as they wish, was a good solution born out of the SNM struggle. And that is one of the reasons that Somaliland is blazing a road much different from what our brothers in Somalia are going through.

Recently, we went through a crisis when the Guurti unilaterally renewed for itself another term. For a self-interested body to do this is a travesty of justice. But, we know the root cause. We haven't yet found a way of electing the Guurti. Before the constitution was passed the members were simply selected by their clans through the traditional system of elders. Now our present constitution says that the Guurti—the upper house of our bicameral system—has to be elected, albeit under a special law. That law has not yet been debated or drafted. Without belabouring the point, I personally do not believe that the Guurti should be elected through a general one-person-one vote system. If this is done it will not be a Guurti, but a replica of the house of representatives.

We have two choices to solve this problem:

- To elect the Guurti on a popular suffrage like the House of representatives, as I said before I oppose this alternative because the Guurti then loses its reason for existence. If we choose the above position the Guurti will be like the American Senate. And then we would need another body to represent our traditional clan system for which we have a sociological need.

- Rather than creating too many bodies which we can hardly afford in our nascent democracy. Let us have the Guurti in its present form but debate seriously how we can reconcile the electoral and the traditional. Let the Guurti represent the latter but find a way where clans can select their representatives in an agreeably equal way. I believe we can find a solution. But, let us be open-minded.

IV- On Islam

It is clear today that there is a Western onslaught on Islam presenting it as backward, anti-human, anti-women, anti-democratic and most recently terroristic. This is nothing new. Long time ago since Europe dominated us, it was the function of so-called Orientalists to present an ideology in which the West is the progressive, logical and rational entity, while we are showed as irrational people who deserve to be ruled, to be civilized. It is enough to read Edward Said's Orientalism to get the picture.

What is new today is the infamous War on terror and the new ideology of "Clash of Civilizations" to justify all types of aggressive and destructive wars from Iraq, Afghanistan, Somalia and other places in order to 'democratize and civilize us through 'Regime changes.' We in the Islamic world who know better realize that this is a dead-end road that leads nowhere for all of us, the East as well as the West. We also know that this so-called "clash of civilizations" is a figment of some peoples' imagination. It has little to do with historical reality. We know that, and they know it too, despite their denials, that it was Islamic Civilization that has revived the Egyptian heritage, the Greek and Roman Civilizations. From Islamic Scholars like Ibn Rushdi and Ibn Khaldun they have learned their heritage when they were in the 'Dark Ages.' Cultures and religions learn from one another and there is no clash, unless artificially created by the imagination.

Genuine Muslim Scholars know better. They not only know the basics of Islam. They also know the history of its development. Those Orientalists, who are sincere, in their study of the Orient, also know that Western Civilization would not be what it is without Islamic contributions. We were their teachers and later they imposed themselves as our teachers. It is not a question of knowledge. It is a question of power. But, still we cannot deny that, after our glorious days, we Muslims declined. Long before European invasion and colonization of our lands we were weakened by internal conflict of many sorts—Sunni against Shia, umawiin against Cabbasiyiin, and later particular nationalisms. What the colonialists conquered was an already weakened Umma by its own conflicts. Now where do we go from here as an Islamic Umma? I myself have no definitive answer. But, certain things are clear: (i) Revival of Islamic morals are necessary. (ii) Democratization of our countries so that in each country it is the voice of the people that is heard and rules. (iii) Co-ordination among the countries themselves, even in their present condition. (iv) Resistance to this onslaught and showing our weight to the world as an Islamic umma.

But, there are more points that have to be said on this issue. There are those among us, feeling frustrated and humiliated, who are lashing out indiscriminately killing innocent civilians, including fellow Muslims, in the name of Islam. I, for one, do not sympathize with those kind of people. These groups and their actions are providing the perfect excuse for those in the West who want to attack us morally, politically and militarily. You can say that they are two sides of the same coin. In saying this we have to distinguish them from genuine resistance movements like Hamas and Hizbullah. Theirs is a true liberation struggle against oppression and they have every right to utilize their faith in strengthening their morale. The ones I cannot sympathise with are those groups elected by nobody, representing nobody, having no country and yet are trying to impose on us their brand of Islam, if Islam it is. The result of their actions only serves and strengthens the oppressors.

Let us not get confused by these demagogues. Our heritage is clear. We have the Quran and the tradition of the prophet(CSW). But, we also have our differences in interpreting these texts and traditions. This is normal. The prophet (CSW) said that differences of opinion in my umma is a blessing[Ikhtilaafu ummattii Rahma]. This is the basis of the "shura" [consensus] because this is how decisions are made in society. We should also remember that the great Islamic legal scholars who codified the sharia laws did that several hundred years after the prophet(CSW) and the khulafa u Rashidin. Of course these legal codes are based on the Quran and the tradition of the prophet. But, they did it through their "Ijtihaad" and they did us a favour. Who said the 'Ijtihaad' is over and done with?

V-On Governance

It is a well-known historical fact that after decolonisation the newly independent African regimes did not go foreword: the economy, after a short spurt of growth, slumped into stagnation and decline in many countries; political freedoms metamorphosed into one-party systems or military dictatorships; the standard of living of the common people deteriorated while few enriched themselves — primarily on public resources; and finally the very security of persons and groups became in danger if they called for correction.

There is no wonder if such a deterioration in the system of governance led to social and political strife: in some cases resulting in peaceful accommodation and transition to a better level, and in others to violent civil wars and sometimes a failure of the state.

Explanations for this atrophy differ. Old colonial ideologues revert to overt racism—Africans are not fit to rule! Dismissing that racism aside many African intellectuals put the blame on the operational domination of the world economy and the strengthening of power in the hands of old colonialists, their new replacements and co-operation with local elites through neo-colonial attachments. I have no quarrel with that explanation. I just believe it is not sufficient. There are other former colonies, especially in Asia, which did well. So, we must also look inward, no only for explanations, but also for further change and improvements.

Needless to says the system of how to run a government: constitutions, political parties, civil service, police, army etc, was imported wholesale at the dawn of independence. The West, from whom we imported the system, had several hundred years to digest it: they had their internal strife's, their revolutions, their inter and intra-wars. The African indigenous systems of rule did not have that chance to evolve. They were destroyed or mutilated by cataclysmic events like the slave trade and colonial subjugation.

It is not a crime to borrow something from a better system. I have said earlier that human cultures interpenetrate one another. But, the importation of a whole system, stock-lock-and barrel, is the problem. Plants do not grow in an inappropriate soil and climate. It was therefore inevitable that historical development after independence would be bumpy until African peoples find the road to their second liberation, each country in its own way. I believe that future historians will regard Somaliland as one of the countries that have blazed the road for the new African regeneration, that is the regaining of the original goals of the decolonisation movement: Liberty with social and economic progress. In the meantime, we have to consolidate our achievements so far, refine them and think ahead in order to avoid continuous crisis.

What I have said so far about the political parties, decentralization, the role of culture and religion is part of the general system of good governance. I want to add only two more points. To confine political parties at the national level to three is sensible. We wanted to avoid the free for all confusion that paved the way for the military coup de tat in 1969. But, that should not mean the creation of monopoly political power to three particular parties only. That will ossify political development and will definitely breed future crisis. There is nothing better than to leave the market of political ideas open, trust our people, whom I consider mature enough, but still limit the number of national parties to a few. How to do it is a matter of detail, which we can achieve, given sincerity and good will.

The other point I want to make in this context is government performance per se, no matter which political party holds the reigns of power.

To consolidate the existing peace and expand justice the government as the guardian of the law must be the first to uphold and abide by it. The checks and balances between the branches of government must be respected, with the independence of the judiciary inviolable.

The executive branch of the government must be lean and clean. We cannot afford huge ineffective bureaucracy which is valued not for its productivity but for its job providing service through nepotism. The main task of the executive, as I see it, is to implement the laws passed by the legislative branch, propose new ones, guide plan and co-ordinate and provide the vision of where to go next [I am, of course, not minimizing its job of providing for defence and security, and conducting foreign policy,] Its job, viewed from the is perspective, shares the characteristics of a teacher. As such, therefore, it must stress quality and assist the private sector, in job creation. However, stressing quality in the civil service and the armed forces should not go to the extreme of neglecting representation. After all we are a nation of clans where unity and justice requires fair representation of the various clans in public affairs and institutions. We should therefore work very hard in combining merit and representation.

The requirement of government to be clean means the struggle against corruption. Needless to say, corruption is a fact of human life in both rich and poor countries, especially the latter, and has been so throughout history. It stems from greed, a bad aspect of human character, which unfortunately gets more pronounced in some of the powerful and wealthy in all countries of the world. However, admitting this fact in no way means submitting to it. Horrible facts can be fought and have been fought like slavery and colonial oppression and have been defeated. So, today horrible facts like poverty and corruption can be fought and overcome. This means that we have to be vigilant.

This vigilance has several means at its disposal. The primary requirement is that all government activities [may be with the exception of concerns of national defence] must be transparent; organs of the executive such as the accounting office, the auditor-general, and the Presidency can first check this transparency. Then by the select committees of both chambers of the legislature. And finally by the public at large, especially civil society organizations and the independent media. Putting such instrumentality into action constantly will reduce corruption, though it may not eliminate it altogether. In all of this the leadership, at all levels, must provide exemplary model.

VI-On the Economy

I am not writing an economic programme. Neither am I writing a party platform. This is a statement of principle by one person. Therefore much will not be said here, except a few points that touch on the principle aspect. There was a prevalent opinion, in the early days of independence, in many African countries that the state should take a leading role in the economy, not only in planning and guidance but in directly productive activities as well. The lack of a middle class who could make the required investment and the success of Soviet-type economies at the time provided the rationale. Some expressed this in terms of some kind of socialistic rhetoric, others in simple statism. But in all, the attitude was overriding. Hence the proliferation of parastatals. The capitalist world, because of Cold War competition, tolerated this approach.

We all know that with the passage of time this did not prove to be a panacea. On the contrary parastatals became inefficient, a breeding ground for nepotism and corruption, and a source oiling dictatorial machines everywhere. The resulting disillusion is inevitable. Then, with the weakening of the Soviet system, and the rise of the right-wing in the West, came what was termed the Washington consensus. This refers to the agreement on global economic policy among the US treasury, the International Monetary Fund, and The World Bank – all in the same proximity in Washington D.C. The essentials of this policy framework were an emphasis on the market and the reduction of the role of government in the economy. The catchwords were privatization, stabilization (i.e. reduction of government expenditures, especially on social services) and open trade. In this view the less regulation the better even after the state auctions off its assets. It was a policy of unbridled capitalism, with which the European Union and other donors, both official and commercial, concurred. It was applied without mercy to developing countries and those in transition from communism to capitalism with disastrous results. Today even the IMF and the World Bank have admitted some of the adverse effects of such policies on the poor and are claiming to revise them. Today we can see with hindsight that both approaches served ideological positions – from the left and right respectively – rather than economic rationality. The experience of many countries – specifically East Asia – has shown that there is a third way. Rather then viewing thestate and the market in antagonistic conflict, they can be seen as complementary. Economic growth requires a vibrant private sector. But, there is also need for strong state policy to plan, guide, and co-ordinate all kinds of economic activity, specially the financial aspect. Also an unbridled market is a greedy machine that rolls over the weak resulting in misery and unacceptable inequalities. Governments, therefore, must look for the public good. That means, not only regulating the market, but also engaging in human development such as health, education and the environment. In our case, this third way is the best option.

VII- By Way of Conclusion

We know we are a poor nation. But, poverty need not be a curse. There are nations with meagre resources like us who overcame poverty. Human development and its mobilization can compensate for the lack of resources and perform miracles. In addition to investing in health and education human development also means instilling solidarity and a sense of belonging to one another, having a common future and destiny, among the citizenry and their various communities and clans. Competition in business, politics and among the communities can be both healthy and unhealthy. If the unhealthy aspect is not fought fiercely it can turn into ugly fratricide [look at the situation in Somalia]. One of the reasons motivating me to write this simple piece is that I noticed from afar that this competition is beginning to turn ugly. Simple matters that can be resolved through amicable discussion and dialogue between the concerned personalities and organs are sometimes turned into unnecessarily highly contested national controversies wasting, when they are finally resolved, a lot of energy and good will.

Let us check that tendency in time. We still have not lost that capacity for good will and democratic dialogue, inherited from the struggle of SNM, which is the basis for the success of Somaliland so far. We need to revive moral values of integrity, cooperation, forgiveness and brotherhood in our people. And while this task is the duty of all of us, the primary burden falls on the leadership: political (whether in power or aspiring to it), religious, community elders, and the intelligentsia. We need to rise above minor squabbles and take the high moral ground. Some of you may say that I am too idealistic and out of touch. I do not think so. I believe what is written here is simple and practical. I am an optimist and have always been so even at dark moments when my life was in danger. Even if these words are idealistic, so be it. After all it is the image of the future that moves people and it is vision that enables a society to organize itself for the better. It has been said long ago that those who do not learn from history are condemned to repeat it. It is my hope and belief that we have learned enough and will continue to move forward.

Wa billahi al-towfiq.

Beyond The Tunnel: The Democratic Practice In Somaliland And Its Future
By Ibrahim Megag Samatar, 2011

Somaliland has been practising democracy in various different forms for the last fifteen years. It can be said that the first phase of democratic practice in Somaliland was based on clan consensus. The different clans resident in the country selected, according to their own methodology, includes the elders who would represent them in the several national conferences that were held for different purposes such as peace and reconciliation, the political future destiny of the country, or appointing further representatives in future working bodies like the Guurti, the House of Representatives, and members of the Government.

Certainly, the system in this phase was not fully democratic. All the clans were not represented. Some, like the Gabooye and other minority clans, slipped through the net without deliberate intention to block them out. Needless to say the patriarchal process totally excluded women. Even some of the clans who were represented may not have been fully satisfied with the system either because they wanted a larger share or the internal distribution of the share itself was considered unfair, and obviously the population at large had no voting rights.

Yet, it could not be called a despotic system. It was not a military dictatorship ala Siyad Barre. The Somali National Movement (SNM) did not behave as a one-party dictatorship, as happened with many armed liberation movements after attaining power; nor was it organized as such. The system also was not a majority clan denying others their rights, as so many have falsely accused the Isaaq of doing. This false accusation was exposed by the 1993 Borame conference where the Samaroon, who were not SNM supporters, played the honorable role of the mediating host.

Despite these anomalies the system in this phase can still be described as democratic because it somehow provided a channel for public opinion to be expressed. In difficult circumstances, the people of Somaliland tapped into the traditional culture of the nomadic system-what the anthropologist I. M. Lewis called pastoral democracy. Most people did not see the imposition of the nomadic system on a modern state as a viable alternative in the long run. They saw it for what it was, a transitional phase.

Today, we can safely say that we have passed that phase with a good grade. A constitution has been drafted, debated and approved in a referendum. Local, presidential, and parliamentary elections have taken place. These elections were not without their faults and defects whether in the planning or execution stages. But, considering our conditions: meager resources, a country whose cities, physical and social infrastructure had been destroyed by a protracted war; a sizeable section of the educated able young people spread abroad in the Diaspora; and just emerging from the most recent armed civil conflict. Considering these conditions, we have indeed done well. Many countries, which did not suffer these traumas, and which receive more assistance than we do, are unable to accomplish as much. This has been attested to by objective foreign observers.

But, this is no reason to rest on our laurels. This second phase is also transitional and incomplete (I will have more to say about the Guurti later on). Some of us maybe as proud of these achievements as to forget the shortcomings and dangers ahead. Others may brood on the defects to the point of gloomy hopelessness. Both these tendencies have to be avoided. The glass is both half-empty and half-full. What is required is a sober summing up of our situation: where we are, how we arrived here, and a vision of the f untrue we hope for, and how to get there. This is a task facing us all, collectively and individually. Allow me to make my modest contribution to that endeavor.

One relevant question is why was it possible for the people of Somaliland to reconcile, lick their wounds and go forward while the brothers in Somalia got enmeshed in a vicious cycle of unending fratricide? I do not claim to have satisfactory answers. Several points, however, come to mind. For one thing the dominance of foreign players in the affairs of Somalia, and the lack of it in Somaliland, could be a factor. How many foreign players have an axe to grind and are totally altruistic? It is an ABC of politics that every power primarily pursues its own interest. Diplomatic arrangements, agreements and political solutions are in a sense, the result of these interactive interests. But, when foreign players do not have a national entity, no matter how poorly organized , as their bargaining counterpart, but instead are facing a melee of factions, clans, warlords (call them what you will) competing for their favor, it is difficult to see a viable national solution as a result of such a process. Even the UN has its own implicitly built-in bureaucratic agenda that has to be confronted by an entity representing the national interest. In such exceptional circumstance the absence of foreign players, at least for a short while, is a blessing.

Secondly, the different colonial experiences may have some relevance. Every colonial experience has a stunting effect on the psyche, personality and structure of the colonized society. But, there may be a difference of degree and not of kind here. The tendency of British imperialism to employ what it called indirect rule may have had a different effect on the structure of society from the practice of Italian fascism. There is no doubt that the employment of community elders by the colonial authorities as tool of their rule had a distorting nature. Yet, we can now see with hindsight, the co-opted elders not only kept some semblance of their leadership, but also formed buffer strata between the colonial authorities and their people. It was through their mediation that the colonial authorities could gauge the impact of their intended laws and measure on the society-and the level of acceptance or resistance-and therefore had an opportunity to modify such rules and measures. In that role the elders performed some protection-no matter how partial-for their people, their culture, religion and their way of doing things. That is why the later emergent groups in urban areas-such as businessmen, school graduates, and politicians-could not totally replace the moral authority of the traditional clan elders. Contrast this with the practice of Italian fascism-and the later Italian rule under the UN Trusteeship which ignored and undermined the traditional leadership. Is it any wonder that, after the failure of the post-colonial state, the people of Somaliland had something to fall back on while those in Somalia ran amok?

Finally, and I think this is the most important, the third factor accounting for the difference is the experience gained by SNM during the liberation struggle. Thirteen years ago, I presented a paper at a Somali Studies Association entitled "Light at the End of the Tunnel: Some Reflections on the Experience of the Somali National Movement." Without repeating what I said then, let me emphasize a few points relevant to our discussion here. I predicted then that Somaliland will with some ups and downs of course, accomplish the tasks of reconciliation, reconstruction and the movement forward toward democratic governance. The basis of my argument was that the qualities required for the accomplishment of such tasks namely compromise through dialogue, power-sharing, self-reliance and resilience during adversity-had already been tested and practiced by the SNM during the liberation struggle. It was a matter of extending the gained experience to the level of Somaliland.

We, in SNM, have been accused on various occasions by both some supporters and opponents of just riding the wave of the armed struggle without a guiding vision. I must admit that I never understood that accusation. Were the accusers looking for some kind of ideological brand or so-called charismatic leadership shining over the rest of the movement? Were thy disappointed by the apparent weak discipline among the ranks and the porous nature of SNM?

Let me remind you, lest it is forgotten, that we were struggling for a democratic rule against a venal dictatorship and the stupidity of so-called charismatic leadership. The regime has imposed a borrowed ideology on the people and we had no intention of repeating that suffocating terror. The weak discipline itself was the price one has to pay for democratic dialogue. All decisions-from top to bottom and in the branches abroad-were made according to the rules of democratic discussion and majority voting. Hence the porous nature of our organization. Imagine the situation if a movement with a particular ideology and ruling with an iron first took power in Somaliland in 1991. The result would have been one of two situations: either SNM imposing its own kind of dictatorship or in case we failed to do so, a free-for-all chaotic conflict as happened in the South (Somalia). I am glad to say that we knew better.

Another point which I want to underline here is the political role of the Guurti. In some discussions of this topic one gets the feeling that the Guurti suddenly mushroomed in 1992, or rose to the occasion after the so called failure of SNM to rule. Aside from the moot point whether a two-year period is sufficient enough time for judging failure or success, let me make an important reminder in history. The political role of the Guurti is one of the most fruitful experimentations of SNM. Some crucial questions presented themselves early on in the struggle: First, how to deal with the issue of clanism during the nation-building in the future; Secondly, how to spread the intended democratic practice beyond the SNM committees and its activists to the supporting population at large. We all recall that during the struggle for independence from colonial rule our clan heritage (called then tribalism) was viewed as a backward anachronism to be cleansed from the structures, laws and norms of the modern stat-to-be. How a long surviving cultural institution can be suddenly discarded while alternative substitutes performing its useful functions have not yet evolved was not asked (if understood at all). An imported political and legal superstructure was therefore superimposed on the traditional substructure, to which the people ascribed in their behavior, attitudes and loyalty. We all know what that gave birth to: a society with a split personality which again gave birth to the Siyad Barre dictatorship.

To avoid a repetition of such a farcical tragedy obviously required an ability to bridge the modern and traditional. I.e. utilizing the best aspects of heritage while adopting to the new. How to minimize the negative aspects of the heritage is a continuous generational struggle. Therefore SNM, representing the nucleus of a modern political institution, and clan leadership had somehow to be brought together in a formal relationship-informal cooperation at the level of the local fighting unit was a must, anyway. First steps at formal organization of the Guurti in 1983 and again in 1985(I chaired the attempt in 1985) did not prove to be permanent, primarily because the effective clan leaders were inside the country, while we were guests in Ethiopia. This gap was filled in 1988 when a substantial majority of the populations of Hargeisa, Burao and Berbera crossed the border as refugees after the destruction of those cities by the regime during the full confrontation between it and the SNM forces. In that year, the elders of the supporting population held a conference in the village of Aderrosh and autonomously organized themselves in the present form of the Guurti. From then on the Guurti Committee attended, as observers, the meetings of the Central Committee of SNM, and vice versa. Thus began the formal co-existence and co-operation of the two sides of the struggle: the modern and the traditional. Finally at the Congress of SNM in 1990 the Guurti was promulgated a constitutional body. And this was the basis of our present bicameral parliament.

But, history moves in zigzags. The actual realization of the vision after Liberation took a somewhat different path. The traditional side of the duality swallowed the modern side. This appears understandable considering the infancy of the modern side, the long-rooted skill of traditional leadership in conflict resolution, and the inevitable appearance of points of conflict in a destroyed post-war society. Thirteen years ago, I argued that this dominance of the traditional side is not a sin if meets the requirement of peaceful conflict resolution. I also predicted that, since dependence on traditional leadership is only a partial solution and is not a substitute for a mature political evolution, the modern aspect of the duality will be revived in due time.

That is how we arrived where we are today. We have certainly come out of the tunnel, but we are not out of the woods yet. This is therefore another occasion to roughly outline a vision that will help guide our actions in the future. Let me say clearly that there is nothing original in what follows because they represent our aspirations. Many of the following points have been made elsewhere by many others. But, it is useful to reiterate them in a summary way at this stage of our development. That we are on the road of building a 'democratic' society is our consensus. But, what do we mean by that?

Let us get some preliminaries out of the way. These days it is very common to present democracy as a value of western civilization and proselytize it as such. Some of us, therefore, reject it and thereby throw the baby out with the bath water. On the contrary, democracy is a human experimentation and arises out of the human condition. Thus while its forms and expressions may vary according to time and place the essential content points to the same need of justice and participation in decision-making. We have seen how our nomadic culture had an essential democratic content. The same is true of sedentary African traditions. We must remember that the phenomenon of a single all powerful dictator relying on military or a one-party machine is a post-colonial product. The typical African chief could ignore the advice of the tribal council only at his own peril.

Moreover, there is the other tendency of juxtaposing Islam and democracy as opposing tenants. We Muslims know better. We know that the achievement of justice (Al-'Adala) and decision-making in common (shuura) are important components of Islam. Let us remember a moment in the 'sirat' of the prophet (peace be upon him) when the Muslims were defeated the prophet (PBUH) himself was wounded. It was a moment of frustration, confusion and despondency. The following verse of the Quran was then revealed.

And by the Mercy of Allah, you dealt with them gently. And had you been sever and harsh-hearted, they would have broken away from about you; so pass over their faults and ask Allah's Forgiveness for them; and consults them in the affairs. Then when you have taken a decision, put your trust in Allah, certainly Allah loves those who put their trust in Him." (Al 'Imran 159)

Here we have in a nutshell the essentials of democratic governance: tolerance, magnanimity, dialogue, consistency, after the dialogue, in the rule of Law. The practical application of these principles is subject to 'Al-Ijtihad' — which is the process of research and experimentation subject to time and place.

The primary task now is to consolidate the achievements, correct the shortcomings and move foreword. The broad view is to recognize the indivisible three-dimensional nature of our democracy: Somali tradition, Islamic faith, and the requirements of a modern state. If in 1993, the swing of the pendulum shifted to the extremity of relying solely on the traditional side, we should now avoid the other extremity of unutilizing traditional leadership. The heavy cost of zigzags can be avoided with the help of foresight. That is why the election of the Guurti according to universal suffrage will be a step backward. The Guurti then will no longer be a Guurti , but a replication of the House of Representatives. The implementation of the constitutional requirement of the election of the Guurti while keeping its essence as representing traditional leadership is the critical issue before us now. This cannot be resolved through the present Guurti handling its own judgment of itself. This would be a travesty of justice. The issue should be as was our custom, resolved through debate and compromise, and then a special law passed as required by the constitution.

Resolving this, however, does not mean that our road to democratic construction is completed. The meaning of democracy is not confined to the election of bodies and persons who would rule (or misrule) us for a number of years. This is only the skeleton, which we have to clothe with flesh and breathe life into it. To be effective in the long run, that is to say constant with development and freedom, our democracy has to also be participatory and transparent. To ensure this requires , in addition to the independence of the judiciary and the media, a full decentralization , internal democracy of the political parties and autonomous professional and non-governmental bodies. Let us look at some of these in turn.

With major decision-making in the center leads to lopsided development. This is a curse in Third Word countries. We already see the beginning of that tendency in Somaliland with Hargeisa towering over the rest of the country. This is not the fault of the people of Hargeisa or a deliberate decision of the Central Government to favor Hargeisa. Uneven development is a systemic matter and must be fought systemically. It would be shameful if we replicate what we rebelled against. The genuine meaning of decentralization is clear: more power, decision-making and resources have to be devolved to the regions and localities. All persons holding positions of responsibility, aside from civil servants, have to be elected. This power to the regions and localities as well as their relationship with the center will have to be elaborated, after debate, in legislation. We have already taken some good steps in this direction which need to be more systemized.

The political parties, whatever their number, must also be decentralized internally democratic. While each party is entitled to have its own rules, regulations and disciplinary measures, there are general matters that need to be legislated such as: membership rights, periodic elections at all levels and rules concerning them, the relationship between the center and the localities and legal procedures in case of disputes. Democracy at the party level is an essential building block of democracy at the national level at large. If members of the party are not able to elect their leaders (at all levels) freely and democratically, then national elections themselves would be tantamount to a farce. This is the responsibility of all present party activists, especially the leaders. Any party that blazes the way in this field (for we all know that this is something new to us) will not only be morally unassailable, but will be building its own future capacity to rule better.

There are many other interlocking issues and factors involved in building a viable democratic society enshrined in the Islamic faith such as the role of economic organizations, professional and other autonomous bodies, morality, and education. These matters as well as foreign relations are not discussed here. Time and space do not allow me to do so. I hope others will. I simply concentrated on the dynamics of internal political development. It is clear that we are at a critical juncture. We have made good progress, despite some setbacks and gained a lot of experience. But, there is still a long way to go and many tasks ahead. I have tried to show what some of these tasks are within the context of our history, culture and faith. The reconciliation, peace and stability, of which we are so proud can be in danger unless they are continuously nurtured and made permanent. This will be difficult if we are unable to deliver the goods in terms of good governance and development. I am confident that with perseverance, tolerance and cooperation, success will be ours. And we have the opportunity to succeed. But if, God forbid, we fail this historical duty then future generations will have to shoulder it, for life's struggles continue. But, then remember, history will judge us very harshly.

Light At the End of the Tunnel: Some Reflections on the Struggle of the Somali National Movement
Ibrahim Megag Samater, 1993

1. Prologue

What follows is not a narrative account of the activities of the Somali National Movement (SNM) since the start of its struggle against the military regime of Siyad Barre. Nor is it an impartial academic evaluation of its performance and impact on Somali politics. It is not an analysis of the Siyad Barre regime or an examination of the role of external players in the Somali debacle. It is none of these and yet it is all of them. It is none of the above because it does not deal with each aspect with the necessary and sufficient depth and extent required for full treatment. It is all of these because these aspects of the Somali tragedy are touched upon in one way or the other.

This presentation is as its title says: reflections. And reflections by their very nature are untidy. They go back and forth in time and cross-sectionally across topics without any predesigned order. In this respect many aspects of the Somali problem are discussed. The zigzags in international policy towards Somalia, together with many false starts, are described. The experience and development of the Republic of Somaliland and its essential difference from the rest of Somalia is brought out. After a digression on the problems of politico-economic processes in Africa, a return is made to critical evaluation of the struggle of the SNM.

But there is method in the madness. In reviewing topics, the connecting thread is to seek those factors that were causal in the decay and destruction of the Somali state and the effect of that destruction on civil society. The seeking for causal factors itself means the identification of those elements essential for revival. In this search for casual factors, the torch light focuses on several dualities: dependence vs. delving inward; authoritarian state power vs. participatory democracy and traditional structure vs. "modern" institutions. Even though

all these dualities are interconnected, there is a contradiction --
complementary spectrum within each duality: in other words,
a dialectical struggle.

There is a parable in Somali children's folklore about a race
between a fox and a tortoise. Both finally reached home. But
the fast fox, in its hurry, met with many obstacles, difficulties,
and twists and turns. We may say that the fox's situation was
a case of more haste and less speed. The tortoise, on the other
hand, was definitely slow, but it reached home with steady and
sure steps and with less damage. Can we take this parable as
an illustration of the choices available to us in social change:
depending on tradition itself for continuity (tortoise) or throwing
the old overboard and welcoming the new with gusto? Or is a
dialectical intermix better than the either/or?

The discussion of such matters in the text is conducted with
specific reference to the practical struggle of the SNM -- as well
as its vision. It is therefore neither a theoretical evaluation nor a
practical account. It has a little of both, but it aims to sum up the
experience in an introductory way!

Finally, I am not impartial. As one of the leaders of the SNM
itself, I cannot be impartial. Irrespective of whether we in the
SNM made mistakes or not, I cannot be impartial to the cause
of liberation against dictatorial despotism and injustice. But this
does not mean lack of objectivity. A partisan for liberty cannot do
without a merciless search for truth. Impartiality is required of a
judge in a judicial case. But historical causes require partisanship
with objectivity.

II. Predilections of Policy

A cursory glance at the confusion and tragic complexity of
Somali politics today may convince the observer -- and sometimes
the participants -- of the impossibility of a solution. Many are
persuaded to throw up their hands in despair. At the same time,
many players plunged into the deep water of Somali politics with
undue haste, only to pop up again and get out without giving the
swim a try.

The pessimist has many points stacked in his favor.

1. The United States, the major power in post-cold war politics, led the international community -- that was moved by pictures of starving children -- into the quick plunge of Operation Restore Hope. The amassed technology, the number of troops, the apparent resolve, the pomp of the military machine, and the glitter of the media -- it was a big show, marvelous to watch. Nation after nation joined the bandwagon and declared its willingness to send troops to Somalia. For the general public of world opinion and specifically that of the United States -- uninitiated in the history and slippery politics of our small nation -- it was as if the international community had at last come of age. The cold war is over and peace is no longer endangered by superpower rivalry. As for local conflicts, the world can act, in a collective, multilateral fashion led by the only remaining superpower, to resolve them or at least contain them and prevent them from spreading and disturbing the larger prevalent peace. The humanitarian consequences of these local conflicts can simultaneously be dealt with in a resolute manner. Thus, the stage was set and Somalia became the prime test of the new interventionist mission[41] --a contradiction in terms or the first installment of newspeak phrases of an Orwellian age -- which became mired in a local civil war, shooting and killing the people it was supposed to save, and destroying their homes. The interventionists just added a new name -- UNIUS -- to the long list of the contesting so-called "Warlords." Finally, Operation Restore Hope ended up -- via UNOSOM II -- in debacle, as "Operation Despair Rescue. "

2. The United Nations Organization, as the depository of the international community's collective wisdom and systems

---

[41] During the visit by President Bush to Somali to raise the morale of American soldiers on Thanksgiving Day and to present the olive branch of the new humanitarian mission to the starving Somalis, some American newspapers printed a story of the appearance of Jesus Christ (to both American soldiers and Somalis!) above a cloud of dust over the small town of Wanlawein. The authenticity of the story is not as important as the timing of the apparition. Have we reached the limits of propaganda gimmicks?

of action, has been bungling the Somali crisis from beginning
to end. The day Siyad Barre was defeated, the UN bodies and
staff fled as if they were part of his regime[42], rather than staying
and performing their expected duty of serving the people. If
evacuation was dictated by reasons of staff security, a rationale
not wholly acceptable, then at least a stop-gap measure and a
plan of return should have been put in place.

In lieu of a consistent policy and line of action, what we have
witnessed on the part of these international organizations led by
the UN is a mass of ad hoc activities moving like a pendulum
from extreme to extreme. From the extreme of total neglect and
abandonment there was a sudden move again to a position
of over-involvement and domination. The mandate was no
longer confined to the traditional functions of the UN and its
related agencies, such as the delivery of humanitarian aid and
peacekeeping. It now included forced disarmament of the factions
involved in the civil war (in other words, direct intervention
which, evidently, cannot be neutral), "guiding" or, to tell the
truth, running the process of reconciliation and attempting to
determine the shape and form of its end product -- a government
of "national unity." The new concept of peacemaking was
coined and the Secretary-General had to work hard to obtain
new resolutions from the Security Council in order to obtain the
empowerment necessary to implement these new burdens. In
the meantime, the UN has to create its own special bureaucracy
-- United Nations Operation for Somalia or UNOSOM -- to carry
on administrative as well as judicial functions, because there is no
"government." In other words, the UN put itself in the position
of a new outside or colonial administrator after the collapse of the
Siyad dictatorship until such time as a government of "national
unity" is created. This aggressive interventionism on the part of
the UN apparatus has been given a jolt by the withdrawal of

---

[42] Whether or not, and how much, international organizations contributed to
the longevity of the dictatorial regime, and to the misery of Somalians, is another topic outside the scope of our present story.

American -- and later other western) troops early in 1994. But despite this shock, up to now, we see no sign of the UN apparatus abandoning its political-interventionism. We see no indication of a broader and wiser policy with a long-term vision to replace the current ad hocism.

3. Last, but not least, the pessimist would point to the abysmal record of the Somalis themselves. For twenty-one long years, they have acquiesced to one of history's most horrible tyrannies. After the first few years of Siyad Barre's "revolutionary honeymoon," the nature of his regime became clear to all. By the end of the Somali-Ethiopian war of 1977 -78, it became evident to all who could think clearly that the continued existence of this regime undermined the future existence of the nation itself. Somalis with conscience foresaw that if the regime were allowed to continue to pursue its policies unchecked, that by the time it is overthrown or it just comes to its natural end, there may be nothing left to save. They were, like the prophet Noah, crying at the deaf ears of their countrymen and the rest of the world, that the monster should be stopped and the monstrosity put to an end.

Yet the reaction of their Somali countrymen was to cooperate in the continuation of their own oppression. They have allowed Siyad Barre to play on the characteristic rivalry of the clans so well that they were willing to be hoodwinked into bribery, cajolement and blackmail, even to bear arms against a so-called hostile clan. The fervent competition for the regime's favor reached such a pitch that any man of integrity who resisted the co-option risked imprisonment, the loss of life and property, or being labeled as a madman. Likewise, any group, clan, or region, attempting to safeguard its rights, protect itself or voice opinions for the better running of the nation's affairs risked genocide by the regime... with the apparently willing cooperation by the rest of the Somali community. It somehow escaped the attention of Somalis that the acquiescence -- if not downright approval and collaboration -- by the rest of the community in singling out a single section, clan, or region for persecution and genocide spelled the same fate for the rest.

Nonetheless, the end of the regime came through a combination of a number of factors. The persistence, to the point of death, of the minority that was leading the armed struggle against it, at last proved that the dictator can be opposed, resisted and finally defeated. The defeat of his army by the militants of the Somali National Movement and the total collapse of the governmental machinery in the North after 1988 encouraged the incipient opposition in the South to be braver. With some help from the SNM, the United Somali Congress (USC), representing the bulk of the population of the center from Galkacayo to Mogadishu and the Somali Patriotic Movement (SPM) of the Kismayo area were able to fan the flames of the armed struggle against Siyad Barre in the south. They were joined by the normally silent, but very large population, west of Mogadishu and all the way down to Kismayo. These people in the southwest, who were under-represented throughout all the regimes, now had the chance to participate in some real action determining their destiny through their organizations -- the newly formed Somali Democratic Movement (SDM) and a southern wing of the Somali National Movement (SNM).

By this time, the Siyad regime was near collapse. True to its nature, the dictatorship was unable to compromise. Whatever carrots it offered were either wrongly delivered, insufficient, or offered too late. Instead, it continued to alienate and antagonize ever newer elements of the society. The clever manipulation of the divisive clan structure of Somali society paid its final dividend of reducing the manipulator to what he really was -- a lonely madman. The international press, at this time, dubbed him the "Mayor of Mogadishu." The loss of the North, and the closure of Berbera port, the main exit port for Somali exports of livestock, put the regime in financial bankruptcy. At this time also, with the horrible massacres of Hargeisa and Burao becoming evident to the whole international community, those governments supporting the dictatorship could no longer do so brazenly and had to terminate their aid to him.

4. Whatever the cause may be, the pessimist would continue arguing -- whether through the sole action of the opposition, whether through erosion of internal and external support, or whether through old age and madness, the dictator was finally pushed out. But did the Somalis seize this long-awaited opportunity to engage, now that Siyad Barre was out of the picture? Did genuine reconciliation efforts pick up the pieces, rebuild the tom social fabric of their society, heal the wounds, and put their nation back on the road? The pessimist would give a clear and resounding NO. He would point to the horrible bloodletting that ensued after Siyad Barre, to the senseless fratricidal war of clans, to the un'ending victimization of the weakest, that finally led to the international intervention mentioned earlier. He would point to the inability of present Somali leaders and the so-called movements they represent, despite all the pushing and promoting of international organizations and friendly neighbours, to come to any sensible working arrangement of their affairs so far. He would point to the adamant refusal earlier in 1989 of the SNM, the use, and the SPM -- the three movements who were conducting the the armed struggle against the regime at the time -- of any and all initiatives ah:ease fire and dialogue between them and the Siyad Barre regime.

These movements, in those days, indicated the futility of any dialogue with Siyad Barre, their unwillingness to grant him on the table what he has. already lost in the field, and argued instead the appropriateness of conducting any dialogue, compromise, and rearrangement of their future by the Somalis themselves outside the framework of the Siyad Barre regime. This looked like more than an empty promise when the three movements made a formal agreement in mid-1990 among themselves on the modalities of their cooperation during the struggle against the regime and after. Specifically, the agreement envisioned that after the overthrow of the dictator, the movement(s) responsible for the victory will form a government of national unity led by, but not necessarily confined to, them Despite the glimmer of hope provided by this agreement, the actual behaviour of the signatory movements at the hour of victory – the pessimist's argument continues -- was quite contrary to the letter and spirit of the agreement. Whatever the politics and internal pressures acting upon them, separately or concurrently, a faction of the USC formed a "government" of its own without consulting its partners and even parts of its most active wings. The SNM declared the separation of the North -the former British Somaliland -- from the rest of the country and formed the Republic of Somaliland. The SPM, for a short while, fought against its former ally, the USC. The description of the subsequent melee need not detain us here.

The pessimists themselves can be considered to be of three types:

a) Those who have given up hope that the Somalis can make their own history, and can come up with a solution to the crisis. This view looks for an outside solution and, in a nutshell, is calling for recolonization, with all the consequences this entails not only for Somalis, but also for the rest of Africa and other Third World countries wherever and whenever local conflicts become intractable.

b) Those who despair of any solution from outside. This point of view considers the Somali clan structure, the political chess game that goes along with it, and the enigmatic nomadic psychology of the Somalis as too much of a puzzle for non-Somalis to tackle. Non Somalis can play only a secondary, complementary role, but the initiatives have to be taken by the Somalis.

c) Those who despair of both internal and external solutions. This point of view u the most dismal -- waits for a miracle to happen. Well, "miracles" n in the sense of the improbable -- do happen. But when they do, they demand as their prerequisite somebody who is willing to take the initiative, and who. despite the tremendous odds, perseveres with an unshakable faith in the pursuance of the vision. "Faith" as the old adage maintains "moves mountains."

Ironically, policy options recommended by the pessimist of the first type are the same as those preferred by the enthusiasts of the new global interventionism. Similarly, policy recommendations resulting from the pessimism of the second type more often than not coincide with isolationist views -- a sort of unrealistic laissez-faire attitude toward international relations. Since one or the other of these attitudes was predominant at anyone time in international circles (as well as in sections of the Somali elites), we should not be surprised at seeing involvement alternating quickly between policy extremes of over-involvement to total neglect that made many of us giddy.

III. False Starts

In this presentation, we differ with all of the above conceptions and viewpoints as well as the lines of action that flow from them. We believe the Somali clan structure, and the politics it reflects, to be no more mysterious than other more or less "ethnic" systems pertaining elsewhere in Africa and Asia. It is a structure that can be studied (and has been studied), analyzed, and understood. As such, it is amendable to policy-making, though not totally malleable as some may think. The cultural, linguistic, and religious homogeneity of the Somali people is not a guarantee against conflict, but helps in understanding and facilitates matters of policy-making. Such analyses and understanding are not a monopoly of Somalis alone. Outsiders, unhampered by clan affiliation, can give objective and impartial analysis and recommendations, provided they have no axe to grind.

Useful foreign contributions to the present Somali crisis in the form of arbitration, encouragement of productive local processes, and material and humanitarian assistance are not only possible, but necessary at this critical stage in which Somali institutions either have broken down or are in an incapacitated state. Foreign players will range from private volunteer organizations, foreign governments, and international bodies acting either in concert or separately, though coordination will always be essential.

Yet despite this need for foreign involvement, the argument that Somalis themselves should provide the key to the solution of their problems is basically correct, simplistic as it appears. Here, the pessimist's second argument -- those who despair of outside contribution -- have more potency than the other pessimist's view -- giving up on Somalis to make their own history. If it is true -- which we hold to be the case -- that Somalis are primarily responsible for their debacle, with some foreign muddling and intervention of course, then the converse must also be true. In other words, the Somalis must also be responsible for the remaking of their society, with some foreign help along the way. Indeed, we would go beyond the "should" and assert that they are capable of doing so.

It is the main import of this article that the Somalis not only are capable of shouldering this responsibility, but are actually doing so even now. The very process of remaking Somali society is going on before our eyes if only we care to look. The tragedy itself and the debacle of the last few years give renewed opportunities for tackling many issues that were either missed or mishandled in the recent history of the nation.

Needless to say, the availability of an opportunity does not guarantee its correct utilization or that the attempt to do so would be successful. This would depend on many factors foremost among which are the attitudes adopted, and actions taken or not taken, by the actors concerned, both domestic and foreign. The point here is that the opportunity exists. If full advantage is taken of this opportunity, chances are that Somali society would be reconstituted for the better and may provide lessons for other societies where "ethnic" conflict threatens the existence of their nations as presently constituted.

The swift alternation between over-involvement and abandonment by the international community creates its own events that in turn produce their own effects and so on. By the time a chain of events plays itself out we are so far removed from the original positions with so much damage done and opportunities lost. Thus, a new drama is played over an already ongoing tragedy, with the result that the deeper undercurrents of the original tragedy are sometimes overshadowed by the new fanfare. It is this atmosphere that creates the present tendency to overrate what is happening in Mogadishu and its surroundings, and generalize it to the rest of the country. The scriptwriters and the dramatis personae of the new drama concentrate on their own scenarios and subplots to the almost total neglect of the themes of the major play. If the overt playing out of certain themes (or scenes) of the original play seem to contradict or threaten their performance, the danger has to be met either by elimination or assuming its non-existence.

Viewed in this light, the total silence on the causes of the Somali tragedy may be understood. The majority of Somali leaders and intellectuals, especially in the South, are not willing to deal with the present crisis as primarily a consequence of the past and, therefore, partly a consequence of their own actions and attitudes. The crisis is viewed simply as a conflict of clans and a struggle of so-called "war lords" over power, after the collapse of central authority and the departure of Siyad Barre. Similarly in the international arena, only the present conflict is discussed as if the genie suddenly popped out of the bottle and can suddenly be put back again if only these "leaders" could be brought together to reach an agreement. Nothing is said about the long years of stifling dictatorship in which the Somali state, social values, and the institutions based upon them were being gradually undermined, a process of destruction in which foreigners wittingly or unwittingly had their share. Nothing is also said about the equally long resistance to this nihilistic rule in which alternative options of organizing society were being tested.

Such questions as to why conflict among the various clans which throughout history was confined to particular localities at particular times, now took this form of gigantic national catastrophe, or why the political factions now existing are purely clan-based, whereas the political parties prior to the 1969 military coup were on the whole built on alliances across clans, are rarely raised, let alone investigated. Somali intellectuals who, on the whole, contributed little to the struggle against the dictatorship, show scarce interest, if any, in investigating the relationship between traditional clan structures and overall political development, or the consequences of politicized clanism. Such investigation would, hopefully, enable us to see whether, and how, the traditional structure can help reshape future institutions of the nation as well as being itself reshaped. Instead, they continue to bemoan the so-called overwhelming role of clanism while their actual behavior is more "clannish" in the political sense, than their ordinary nomadic clansmen. And to their final shame, they advocate shifting the responsibility of reconstructing their society to the international community, a recommendation which is only a measure of their own bankruptcy as a group.

This lack of seriousness breeds animosity to radical departures from the beaten path. We have mentioned earlier that during the reign of the Siyad Barre dictatorship any group raising opinions for the better running of the nation's affairs were marked out for persecution, while the rest of the population either acquiesced or cooperated in that persecution. The international community also adjusted itself to that atmosphere and cooperated accordingly. The present unwillingness to dissect the legacy of that regime or the hostile attitude adopted towards those who refuse to go along with the conspiracy of silence may be considered as a continuation of those previous attitudes. The road of self-analysis and self-correction was never paved with roses. It is always easier to repress painful matters and avoid going along uncharted territory, even though the correct path may be staring us in the face.

IV. The Unique Case of Somaliland

A most revealing illustration of this suppression of relevant matters is the almost total omission by the Secretary-General of the UN in his reports to the Security Council of the Republic of Somaliland and what is happening there, as if it did not exist. On the contrary, understanding the almost lonely and heroic efforts of the people of Somaliland at reconstruction as well as the reasons for the break away holds a major key to the larger riddle of Somalia. Several impartial observers have pointed to the relative stability of Somaliland. Inheriting a totally destroyed country, with almost nothing to build on, the people of Somaliland began literally to pull themselves up by their own bootstraps. They avoided major internal conflicts and man-made famines. Today, they feed themselves, have one of the lowest malnutrition rates in Africa, and are putting in place the future edifices of a viable system of governance.

In the south, in contrast, the major destruction took place after Siyad Barre fled and not in the struggle against him. Attempts at reconciliation most often give way to renewed waves of conflict, and famine, mainly man-made, reached the huge proportions that "justified" the intervention. Here, in this contrasting situations of two parts of the same previous country, may lie a lesson. Instead of studying the relevant success of Somaliland, encouraging it and drawing conclusions that may be of use to the south, as well as to the future of the whole, we find, on the part of both the southern elite and international bureaucracy, an unreasonable animosity towards Somaliland. Instead of giving a helping hand, the UN bureaucracy is bent on destroying Somaliland and nullifying the efforts of its people, as if a cancerous growth has to be eradicated. The southern elite, on their part, repeat phrases on the sacredness of Somali unity and the inviolability of the territorial integrity of the former Somalia, while their own backyard is burning.

Be that as it may, being misunderstood, isolated, or persecuted is nothing new to the Somali National Movement (SNM) and its leaders.

As the political movement which bore the brunt of the struggle against Siyad Barre, it has learned how to deal with persecution, vilification, and isolation. As the political organ that gave birth to the democratic experimentation in Somaliland, and is still guiding it in more ways than one, it has learned how to forgive, how to compromise and accommodate, and how to relinquish state power when this is dictated by the principles for which it Was struggling, even at the temporary cost of its own internal unity. While the so-called "war lords" in the South are at each others throats, the Somali National Movement (SNM) did not find it difficult to transfer state power even prior to the disarmament of its liberation forces and the armed militia of other clans who opposed it during its guerrilla warfare against the military dictatorship.

I can recall no other example of a liberation movement which won power through the barrel of the gun and which was simultaneously so uninterested in ruling with its gun. Even in those cases where the movement concerned was serious about the democratic transformation of society, elaborate measures were taken after victory to ensure that the victor in the armed struggle also remained so in the peace. This was done as if the accomplishment of the required social change could only be performed by that particular organization and no other. The result of this type of political engineering is the ossification of the revolutionary movement and the gradual loss of its originally genuine support. A good example of this type of development is the FLN in Algeria. In other cases, the victor in the revolutionary armed struggle refuses the participation as partners of other actors who were in the field -irrespective of whether they were acting in parallel for the same goal or in opposition.

Sometimes it so happens that some sections of the society are unorganized during the struggle and support neither side. The victorious revolutionary movement then interprets that dormancy as tacit support to the enemy who now lost. This section now comes under suspicion and is prevented from acting as partners in the new democracy; The result in the two latter cases is an invitation to a new round of civil war either in the early stages of the victory itself or in the ensuing later years as a reaction to the increasing monopolization of power by the victorious group. In countries .where political organizations are more or less coterminus with ethnic groups, the explosiveness of this kind of situation needs no emphasis. Such may be said to be the case in Mozambique and Angola, where the ruling groups and the opposition are now in the different stages of learning the process of conflict resolution through dialogue after a lengthy period of painful fratricide.

The new experiment in South Africa, where the leading liberation movement, the African National Congress, came to power through a process of dialogue and reconciliation with its former enemy, is a promising, though untested, development. It augurs well for the future as a promising, less violent means of achieving freedom, justice and democracy. All men of goodwill cannot but congratulate and wish well the leaders of the ANC and others involved in this new experiment. Certainly, the ANC is not a newcomer in the struggle for justice. It is almost a century old and certainly much older than many liberation movements that came to power before it did. It therefore has accumulated plenty of experience, both of its own unique struggle and that of others, that can allow it to chart a new road. Specifically, the pitfalls suffered by the peoples of Africa who, after gaining freedom from colonial rulers did not realize true liberation but slipped back into the darkness of dictatorships and misery, are very instructive. That the monopolization of power by the successful movements played a critical role in the retrogression to the abyss cannot escape the attention of the newcomers.

I have no intention of putting the SNM on the same pedestal as the African National Congress. Certainly in terms of age, the long accumulated experience, the complexity of the issues involved in its past and present struggle, the importance of the country and theater in which it is operating, as well as the stature of its leadership, the ANC is a giant. Moreover, a lot of political organizations (liberation movements as well as established political parties) are eclipsed into dwarfs. In a comparison of this sort, the SNM would appear as the dwarf of the dwarfs. It belongs not only to a small country, but its support can be considered to be based mainly on one clan of that small country. It has no particular ideology that can, despite the smallness, give it luster. And in terms of leadership, it is a listless movement.

Some may even go further and accuse the SNM of being a visionless movement, without a program, without a disciplined cadre, and thus incapable of forming a cohesive administration that would fill the void. These critics would point to the record of its administration after liberation. From 1991-93, the paralysis and the civil strife caused the people to lose patience. They replaced the SNM's administration in early 1993, despite the wishes of the then existing leaders of the SNM.

Such criticism, we maintain, takes a superficial stand. It confuses the personalities of the leadership with the organic nature of the movement. On the contrary, we are here arguing that in these seemingly negative qualities lie the greatness of the SNM. As a movement that primarily drew its support from the narrow base of a clan it succeeded in bringing down the strong edifice of the national dictatorship. The so-called lack of ideology gave it independence and resilience. The absence of "charismatic" leaders and disciplined cadre is one of the ways in which it avoided the build-up of dictatorial tendencies within itself. If the Republic of Somaliland today enjoys relative stability within the context of conditions in the Horn of Africa, then we need to try to understand why. If the people of that small country are surviving through self-reliance, despite international boycotts and deliberate sabotage, then one should try to determine how they are doing it. And if the Somalilanders have found ways to reconcile their differences and reconstruct their society, then perhaps the rest of Somalia would benefit from knowing how it has been done.

The two parts of the former Somali Republic, i.e., the former British Somaliland and the former Trusteeship territory of Somalia, have had the same historical experience since their independence and union in 1960 until the overthrow of the last government of Siyad Barre. Could the different reactions of the two parts to the breakdown of the United Somali state be due to their different colonial experiences under the British and the Italians? Maybe, for the differential impact of the two colonial systems on the underlying traditional structure could have had different consequences. Could the different reactions be due to differences in the underlying traditional structure and cultural values? Unlikely, since the points of similarities in the Somali cultural milieu, irrespective of geographical location, overwhelm points of differences. But before one delves into that distant past, it is certainly more fruitful to look into the most recent past which just merges into the present.

While we do not deny whatever influences the above-mentioned factors may have, we maintain that the relative success of the Republic of Somaliland, as well as its weaknesses, are primarily due to the experience of the SNM in the struggle against the Siyad Barre dictatorship. How it handled (or mishandled) issues at hand; how it utilized or missed opportunities; and how obstacles either enriched or obscured that experience are all part of the essential record of achievement. If self-reliance, internal democracy, and resolution of problems through dialogue and compromise are the characteristics that today differentiate Somaliland from Somalia, it is because these qualities were learned and practiced by the SNM in the heat of the struggle for liberation. If it were not so, it would not have been easy for the movement to offer the hand of reconciliation to those who did not support it even prior to total victory. Nay, it would not have been easy for the militants of the movement to give safe passage to those Somali ex-refugees from Ethiopia who, through an ironical mutation of history, became part and parcel of the apparatus of the dictatorial regime and who, for all intents and purposes, replaced their former hosts.

V. Perspectives on African Development

In order to understand the experiences gained by the SNM during the struggle and to put these experiences in broader perspective it may be more useful to consider some issues fundamental to the crisis of underdevelopment in African countries. These broader issues impinge upon both economic policies and the system of governance at large. The failure of most African regimes, after the euphoria of the first few years following independence, in both economic performance and the democratic governance of their peoples, compel re-thinking these issues. For our purposes, these issues can be formulated as:

1. What is the most appropriate way to forge a nation? Is it through forcing a centralized state machinery or through the voluntary associations of the existing components of civil society?
2. What is the interplay between "modern" national institutions, such as political parties and state bureaucracy and traditional structures such as clan (ethnic) systems?
3. To what extent should one look inward or outward for the solution of one's problems?

These issues can be restated as the questions of dictatorship vs. democratic development, centralization vs. autonomy and self-reliance vs. dependency. No matter how they are phrased the essence remains the same; and the answering of one issue in a certain manner sets the pattern . for the rest and forecloses other paths of development.

It is a well-known story that in the early decades after independence African governments pursued a statist approach in politico-development matters which relied heavily on foreign borrowing, not only capital and technical help, but even ideas and sometimes wholesale institutions. Since economic growth, as such, was perceived to be the magic key to the problems of development and since Africa lacked an experienced capitalist class with the wherewithal to carry on the process, the initiative was shifted to the state. The attraction of this approach to the new ruling elites was further increased by the example of the Soviet model where an apparently former backward country has succeeded in transforming itself through utilizing the state machinery.

The very words used, and naturally still in use, such as "development" "modernization," and "progress" assume moving from one stage to another. For the development experts of the time, and their African pupils, who were molded by the same educational process, this meant, implicitly if not explicitly, the attempt to emulate the attributes of the "developed" West. The attributes to be emulated include, of course, the political institutions, to the extent possible. The consequent development strategy thus gave scant attention to the real complexities of the societies that were to be developed. It goes without saying that, according to this attitude, African indigenous values and institutions are inimical to "development" as they are rooted in "backward" conditions. The corollary that development policy should be pursued, in spite of the people, follows immediately. The result of this attitude is the transformation of development policy into, in the words of a famous African writer, "an epic struggle, of the very few who know, to manipulate or coerce the many who are ignorant into a new and better mode of being in spite of themselves." Needless to say, all this obviates the essential in development, which is the learning process of the majority of the people. The sustainability of the development process in the longer run can be ensured through the commitment of the people to, their participation in, and their internalization of the requirements of that process.

But the state machinery available to Africans on the eve of independence was a colonial product, born out of a long history of oppression and ill-suited to purposes of genuine self-development. This colonial state was viewed by our people with suspicion, and rightly so.

They took refuge in strengthening communal and kinship systems. Hence the divergence between the interests of the state and its machinery on the one hand and that of civil society on the other. We know too well that during the early years of the euphoria of independence we did not question the relevance of the inherited state machine to our goals. Thus, we did not attempt to qualitatively transform it, but simply adopted it wholesale. Lacking the experience of its predecessor and burdened with an ever-increasing role, the new African state tried to fill the lacunae through expansion. Unable to deliver the goods and thus obtain compliance through meeting the genuine demands of the people, it tried to elicit such compliance through compulsion. With the degeneration of the early democracies into empty shells, authoritarian methods, one party systems, and military dictatorships became the rule. Because their authority is not based on the consent of the governed, these authoritarian regimes are, in fact, less authoritative. They, therefore, become increasingly concerned with short-term security matters rather than long-term development. Is there any wonder, then that the situation today in Africa is generally characterized by stagnation, corruption, repression, resistance, civil wars, and mass starvation?

The challenge to all Africans for the last decade and a half has been to pioneer an alternative path of development that leads away from this impasse and opens the door to real progress. Among the clear lessons is the realization that the present crisis in Africa is not only about economic matters but, on the contrary, involves larger political and moral issues. Overcoming the inhibiting legacy of the colonial state compels an inward looking perspective that examines the present society and its mores for ways of transforming it. The first requirement in this self-examination for an alternative path is to find creative political initiatives for eliciting the necessary participation of the people. We have already seen the limits of elitist forms of democracy, i.e., those who imitate the West, as well as coerced forms of "mass mobilization" that only endorse what has already been decided by an authoritarian state. In fact, these are not two different and opposing forms of organizing society. On the contrary, they finally converge in the form of the authoritarian African state. This is not surprising since the content of both types is the dictatorial way of deciding for the people.

Both forms, i.e., elitist corruption of democracy and "socialist" coerced "mass mobilization," breed cynicism, further alienation from the state, and withdrawal into pre-colonial communal and kinship ties. These traditional structures themselves, have been affected by their long relationship with the colonial authorities. They cannot be considered pure. Yet they still command loyalty and respect. What is therefore required is an approach that integrates this cultural heritage into the formal political structure of the state. The state and civil society need not be hostile and juxtaposed entities. Instead democracy must be planted on the

African soil. The specific forms of this democratic regeneration and the specific pathways to it -- whether peaceful or violent -- will vary according to the situation and the circumstances, but the need and necessity for it is clear.

Also certain broad features -- common to all working democracies -can be outlined. First, there must be a limit to the arbitrary authority of the all-powerful state. Second, economic and political power must be shared and diffused throughout society, both horizontally and vertically. Third, the rule of law must be paramount and replace the whims of the holder of power. If these features appear to be the tenets of Western liberal democracy whose imitation by Africans we have considered to have failed, this should not be surprising. Indeed, we consider these broad features to be the essential contents of any democracy. It is the forms and the specific working details that differ according to the existing social context. It is easily forgotten, though Africanists all the time remind us, that pre-colonial Africa, surviving today somewhat in communal traditions, was rich in these broad features of a democratic society. After all, the all-powerful dictator, equipped with an impersonal machinery presides over the fate of society is a post colonial product. In pre-colonial Africa, councils of elders, chosen through lineage hierarchy or other means of popular suffrage, prescribed the powers of the ruler -king or paramount chief, where there was one. Rules elaborated through wide discussions and codified in cultural heritage, religion, custom, and laws circumscribed the conduct of all -- young and old, rulers and ruled.

The integration of these democratic practices and values into the institutions of the modern state must start at the lowest rung. It is at the village level (where normal administration, social services, development programs and political matters can hardly be distinguished) that the training of the common people as citizens should begin. Freely chosen representatives at this level could form the first steps of a pyramid culminating at the national level. It is at the village, district and provincial levels that the communal, clan, ethnic interests can be coordinated, reconciled and combined with that of the nation at large. Traditional leadership structure goes down to the roots and can tap grass roots support. But if not corrected or complemented by cross-sectional political organization -- in other words where leadership does not depend on ethnic/clan loyalty alone -- then it is likely to give way to divisive and centrifugal forces.

The above general remarks apply with particular force in the case of the Somali Republic. Inheriting two disparate colonial experiences, great -- and commendable -- energy was spent in the early years in integrating the different political, legal, administrative and educational systems. A liberal constitutional parliamentary democracy was adopted. However, this attempt at creating the new nation was based not only on the inherited centralized structures of the colonial state but strenuous efforts' were applied to transplant all the institutions associated with liberal, democracy and move away from the traditional clan structure. The latter as a pre-colonial institution, was considered primitive, anarchic, divisive, with potential for savage clan-based fratricidal wars. As such the traditional system was perceived to be the number one enemy of the goals "'l of national independence, i.e., social and economic progress, freeing the individual from the shackles of the ascriptive bonds of tradition, and' fostering instead the foundations of. the institutions of "modern" nationhood with which free individuals can identify. (I recall, as an active member of that special "tribe" of high school students, how in those days we despised everything that had anything to do with "clanism" and how emotional we were about matters of "nationalism" and "independence. ")

Indeed, attack on tradition was an integral part of the independence movement. Despite the veneer of seeking freedom from the colonial yoke and its consequent domination of many aspects of social life, the independence movement imbibed more values from its colonial metropolitan adversaries than it rejected or wished to change. This should not be surprising. Aside from whatever brainwashing there was as a result of educational molding, nationalism, as an historical movement, was a European phenomenon. Moreover, the concept of nation-building, prevalent in those days and paraded as the quintessence of research by political theorists, is the ideological heritage of Western post enlightenment.

The Somali Republic like many others in the African continent, failed in transplanting the liberal state. With the benefit of hindsight, this is also not surprising. Traditions die hard, no matter what strenuous efforts are expended in creating the new. After all, the cultural heritage of a people cannot suddenly be revamped. Institutions that have served a purpose for generations cannot just be outlived unless and until an alternative is found that better serves those same social needs. Otherwise they will continue to exist, albeit sometimes in a corrupted and destructive form. The new laws and institutions of the liberal state could not easily and quickly replace all traditional ones. Implicit in the concept of the liberal state and its laws is the assumption that society consists of free individuals, with basic rights and endowed with different talents. This assumption underlies the rules of equality and even the ballot, the sine quo non of a liberal democracy, is based on that assumption.

One need not quarrel with these assumptions of liberal democracy. They are indeed necessary, but not sufficient for full democratic expression in African countries.

The missing link between the state and the individual is an intermediate category where the bonds of solidarity and human fraternity, so much neglected by liberalism but indeed essential for human survival and welfare, are nurtured. If in the industrial world this warmth of human solidarity and fraternal bonds is sought in organizations based on class, in the less developed world, specially in Africa, they are easily provided in ready-made form by ethnicity in the Somali case by "clanism." The extended family in the Somali case is the basic economic unit, adopted and adapted throughout the ages for the survival of its members. One family member may be a skilled worker in town, another a merchant, a third abroad in Europe or oil-rich Arabia, and another left to tend livestock in the hinterland. All their incomes buttress one another. As such the Somali extended family is a versatile system that is self-reliant, internally balanced and autocentric.

The Somali clan structure is a complicated pyramid with the extended family at its lowest form and a large, more or less political group claiming to originate from a single ancient ancestor at its pinnacle. Subclans in the middle echelons of the pyramid are most often more important for questions of survival and interest. I have no intention to go into a treatise about Somali clan organization and its functions. The simple point being raised here is that sometimes the extended family system may not have the carrying capacity to fully provide for the needs of its members in terms of security (economic and otherwise), emotional support and simple social interaction. Upper rungs in the pyramid are therefore called upon to supplement the efforts and resources of the extended family. The more difficult the problem to be solved in both extent and intensity, the higher the rung called upon. Most often the most important rung in these matters is the diya-paying unit of the clan. This is the unit that is responsible for injuries caused unto others by its other members. The other layers of the clan structure, most often dormant, are activated at times of stress, civil wars, famines or liberation struggles. In urban areas services that are normally provided in industrial countries by the state, municipalities, trade unions, cooperatives, etc., now become the function of the extended family and/or the clan in African countries. The need for clan solidarity, although assaulted in many ways by urbanization, becomes strengthened by it.

The consequence of these contradictory forces -- the inherited colonial state and the liberal laws adopted wholesale on the one hand, and the continuing need for clan support and solidarity on the other -- is a bifurcated society, with a non-integrated personality. This bifurcation is a breeding ground for corruption, misuse of power, manipulation of clan loyalty, mistrust among the clans themselves, and hence instability. The resulting disillusionment, right on the heels of the euphoria of independence, provided the fertile soil for the African coups. Whether, given sufficient time, these contradictions could have been overcome peacefully and democracy could have been workable is one of the "ifs" of history. The fact remains that in the case of Somalia the Siyad Barre military dictatorship came and completed the job of total disintegration. How it did so is an important subject by itself and need not detain us here.

VI. The Experience of the Somali National Movement Reviewed

The resistance to the dictatorship was affected by this historical background in more ways than one. The terror unleashed by the regime, the abolition of national representative institutions, and the transformation of the remaining state bodies into instruments of oppression and spying, left the extended family and the related clan network the only relatively safe haven. While this clan network had already, prior to the regime, built-in advantages for political organization, the behavior of the terroristic regime made it the only avenue for any opposition to it. Further, the clandestine nature of any opposition to the police state of Siyad Barre and the latter's manipulation of the clan structure, setting one clan against another, not only inhibited the building of bridges between incipient opposition groups, but succeeded in the displacement of any resentments against the regime into aggressions against other clans.

Those who criticize the SNM for not starting off with a broader clan base, minimize this factor. There is no need here to recount in detail the efforts of the SNM to do so. These efforts did not materialize in substantial success in the early stages and are witness to the depth of the disintegration process wrought by the regime. Several factors are at play: the smaller bases of support in the center and the south of the country opened by the SNM in the early years; the modus vivendi with the SSDF before the latter's slip into dormancy; the active coordination and subsequent alliance with the use and SPM; and finally the reconciliation process embarked upon on the eve of victory with those northern clans who opposed it all speak with eloquence of the sincerity of these early SNM efforts to broaden its base, despite the odds.

In the meantime the movement had to continue its work where it was most effective vis a vis the north of the country. The single-minded support given to the SNM by the Isaaq clan speaks only of the unevenness of the regime's oppression and its singling out of this clan in the mid and later 80s for particular persecution. The numerical strength of their support, and the uninterrupted nature of their habitat in the North, provided the SNM with ample opportunity not only to continue the valiant struggle with tenacity but also to experiment with ideas and forms that could lay the basis for alternative paths of governance and development. These forms and ideas, needless to say, were not ideological recipes, prepared by elites in the ivory tower, and experimented on an unsuspecting population. Rather they grew out of the practical needs of the struggle itself.

This does not mean that the struggle was visionless. Vision, there has to be. Otherwise it is almost impossible to move great numbers of human beings into action. The tremendous odds against which the SNM operated and the sacrifice it demanded from its supporters over an extended period of time could only be sustained by a vision of the future in which they believed. Some cynics maintain that hate also can move masses of people into action. They point to the Nazi movement, whose effectiveness has threatened the world for sometime, and the ever-present ethnic massacres in today's world. But, evidently, this cynical argument cannot be taken seriously. For one thing, occasional jacqueries should not be confused with sustainable movements. And those sustainable movements that have a large element of hate in their arsenal show it in their expressions and actions. The SNM definitely passes that test. As the saying goes, the proof of the pudding is in the eating.

The vision itself (from which programs of action are formed) is a mixture of ideal and the antithesis of the system one is attempting to change. Certainly hatred of the oppressive system and those who actively and willingly maintain it forms part of the driving motives of the fighter for change. But this is quite different from the kind of hatred alluded to by the cynic, for it is not directed against a particular ethnic group of tribe/clan or section of humanity. It is directed against an oppressive social structure whose removal is a milestone towards realizing justice. For this to be achieved it has to be accompanied by the articulation of the alternative, even if that articulation does not fall into any of the known ideological molds.

We have seen, in the preceding pages, that the oppressive system that evolved in Somalia --and the rest of Africa in various different ways - was characterized by an excessively centralized, dictatorial state, divorced from the traditions and historical continuity of the people it ruled. We have also touched upon the outlines of an alternative form of governance; one that integrates the state with civil society, is democratic and auto centric and decentralizes the arenas of action as much as possible.

This, precisely, is the vision which the Somali National Movement presented from its inception in its programs of action and which it attempted to practice while still conducting the armed struggle against the military regime. If this alternative vision was not very well-known ~, outside its ranks, it speaks less of the limited ability of the SNM to propagate this vision than of the blinders inhibiting outsiders to see the actual truth. I say this with confidence, because even if we lacked the resources with which we could compete with the government in the propagation of our ideas, our actions and activities were an open book for" anyone taking the pains look. Let us now take some of the main elements" of the alternative path, discussed earlier, and which also inform SNM's vision and see what role these ideas played in the praxis of the SNM during the phase of the armed struggle.

If one were to single out a phenomenon in which the SNM is unique among liberation movements, past and present, it is the extent of its self-reliance. To be sure, all genuine liberation struggles have to strive for a measure of self-reliance if they are to achieve success. But, more often than not, it is almost impossible to do without some form of external support in terms of moral and material assistance. Specifically it is the material support that becomes a sine qua non in the case of armed struggles. To mobilize, train, supply, replenish and maintain fighting units is a very expensive affair. Expensive also, if only slightly less so, is the political wing with its far-flung cadres, internally and externally. A liberation movement, conducting an armed struggle, can hardly meet the total of these financial burdens from its own coffers. But the more it relies on external support for the sustenance of its operations and organization, the more it sacrifices its autonomy and independent decision-making. The tendency to be autonomous and independent and the need to seek outside support and allies and thus be part of a larger block is a contradiction that has plagued liberation movements throughout history. Rare is the movement that has found a judicious balance.

The SNM solved this dilemma by tilting towards total autonomy and facing the consequent risk. To be sure the SNM received assistance from Ethiopia in the form of sanctuary for its leadership, training bases for its fighters, and ammunition and fuel. Financial assistance from Ethiopia was next to nothing and even the ammunition and fuel were token contributions. Although this assistance was vital, especially in the early stages, in the long term it was small. The more valuable assistance from Ethiopia was the provision of sanctuary, not the material aspect. This help itself was not a one-way street. The presence of Somali opposition to the Siyad Barre regime in Ethiopia preempted the converse, while at the same time weakening the main threat to Ethiopia from the east. This mutual advantage had the additional strength of sowing the seeds of future peaceful cooperation between the two countries, instead of the then existing antagonism. Sensing this advantage, the Ethiopian regime was wise enough to avoid alienating the SNM by manipulation as much as the latter was careful in insulating its decision-making to itself.

In that Ethiopia was the only source of external assistance, the movement had to provide its own resources or perish. There was, of course, no lack of potential helpers. But the premium put on independence was such that the movement chose to eschew any and all aid that seriously affected its independent decision-making. The harm caused by Libyan cash to the sister and older movement -- The Somali Salvation Democratic Front (SSDF) -- was a clear enough warning. This choice of self-reliance by the SNM paid its dividends. It was compelled to raise cash from supporters abroad and inside the country. The fighting units were to be sustained by supporters in the areas where they operated. Foreign branches engaged in propaganda and diplomatic activity had to rely on their own resources.

All this meant that the rank and file as well as ordinary supporters could no longer be passive sympathizers. Instead, they were transformed into active participants. Thus the path of self-reliance easily led to the road of democratic decentralization. The people whom the movement were trying to recruit and commit to the struggle were already rebelling against a suffocating dictatorship. If they are to be convinced to give the best they have, even their lives, to the cause, they cannot be denied the freedom of choice within the movement. The people have to "own" their movement. One cannot claim to struggle for liberty and deny that liberty itself within their own ranks.

In the context of the struggle conducted by the SNM, the democratic practice expressed itself on two levels: (I) at the top organizational level where the higher leadership -- the Chairman, Vice Chairman and the Central Committee -- were elected in broadly representative Congresses, and (2) at the local level where branches in foreign countries and in the field put forth their own leadership. The most pressing matter is the relationship between the center and the localities. The centralization/decentralization paradox bedevils not only liberation movements but most Third World governments as well. Central authority is a must if a nation has to exist as one. But how much power and responsibility should be devolved to lower bodies, outlying regions and the private sector, and how much power should be retained by central authorities, in order to attain a measure of both democracy and unity is a question not easily resolved. In the case of the SNM struggle, the wide geographic distances involving branches in many countries and field operations across the width and breadth of the country as well as reliance on own resources dictated autonomous activity and decision-making. This left for the center tasks such as broad policy formulation, overall coordination of the implementation, and contact with foreign bodies.

Since particular areas were more often than not occupied by particular clans or subclans, the policy of the movement's autonomous activity in reality translated itself into clan autonomous activity. We have seen in the earlier sections of this article that the post-colonial state failed to integrate traditional authority positively into the modem institutions of society. We have also briefly argued that this divorce between the state and civil society reached an extreme form in the former Somali Republic. Here, the solution to this dilemma of modem versus traditional authority presented itself before the movement in clear form by the exigencies of, the struggle. Ironically, the clan organizational form became the vehicle for a revolutionary process of restructuring society. First, the solidarity it 'naturally provides became a safe haven for members from the state terror. Second, self-reliance itself means that the movement, instead of relying on outside supporters, relies on its people and hence on their local leaders and ways of doing things. There is a mutual feedback here between the movement and the ordinary peoples. The movement brought urban cadres -- the teacher, the army officer, the student, the medical doctor, the politician -- into the rural areas who then interact with the clans and their elders. Here, at the level of the fighting unit, the SNM found the opportunity of integrating traditional authority and methods into the democratic practices and needs of the movement.

These factors created opportunity to correct the mistakes of the past, make use of existing structures, and correct the divorce between civil society and the state. One of the tentative ideas that came about then was a greater role for the elders of the clans as autonomous decision-makers, and participants at various levels of the clan pyramid, parallel with and interacting with the various levels of the formal organization of the movement. The experimentation with the role of the elders was finally formalized in the form of the "Guurti," that is, the senate or the council of elders, which is co-equal with the Central Committee, the legislative organ of the SNM. This parallel co-participation stretched from the lowest units all the way up to the highest level. We see, then, that the vision of an alternative path of governance replaced the centralized, dictatorial regime. The SNM provided an alternative system whose hallmark is participatory democracy from top to bottom. It was thus possible for it to carry over this tradition to a national level after victory, providing avenues for dialogue and compromise while state structures were still weak, culminating in the fora for consensus building such as the Borama Conference. And it is this that makes the vital difference between Somali land and the rest of Somalia.

If there is any weakness in the performance so far, it is that the insistence on free decision-making and participation at all levels has sacrificed the need for discipline and obedience. This has weakened the formal organization of the SNM as a political organ. If this choice has enabled it to escape the appearance of dictatorial tendencies and "war-lordism," it has allowed the formal structures of the movement, as a political organ, to be diluted and absorbed by the traditional structures. Admittedly then, the experimentation for new forms has gone to the other extreme, tending to open the door for centrifugal forces since traditional structures by themselves cannot form the basis for a modern state. But this danger is not as great as it may appear to those who are not familiar with the depth of the changes wrought by the SNM struggle. It is precisely the decentralized forms and the actual democratic participation, especially that of clan elders, opened by the SNM that have minimized conflict within the SNM -- supporting Isaaq clans and between them and the others in the North by institutionalizing dialogue and compromise. Unlike the SNM, the other political factions in the south claiming legitimacy neither opened up such avenue s of activity (at least on a stage comparable to that of the SNM) for the people they claim to represent, nor even conducted formal democratic congresses to legitimate their own leadership. Hence their inability to contain the situation after the breakdown of the Siyad Barre regime, let alone move it forward.

Moreover, those of us who are still optimistic enough to believe in progress also know that trends are never on a smooth, straight line. Like the business cycle, there are troughs and peaks, but the trend is upward with today's trough possibly higher than yesterday's low. If the abhorrence of the dictatorial centralized post-colonial state created in those who thought it a tendency toward too much freedom and reliance on the informal networks, I say proudly that this is good. There was need to restore these networks and legitimize them formally just as freedom was essential. With these firmly established the pendulum will swing back towards formal cross-sectional organizations. Reactivation of the SNM organization is a relatively easy matter and together with those other political organizations that are bound to come up in the present free atmosphere, political alliances across clans will be formed. The need is there and the ground work of dialogue and compromise has already been laid by the struggle of the SNM.

VII. Epilogue

The reader may be struck by the fact that I have said nothing about the important issue of dialogue and reconciliation between the north and the rest of the country, or more precisely, between the Republic of Somaliland and the original Somalia (i.e. the Trusteeship Territory before independence). It is not an oversight, but a deliberate omission, the reasons for which are simple.

First, if by reconciliation, we mean a return to the original union between the two parts, I am afraid it is now counterproductive to harp on that tune. Every problem, like an organism, goes through certain stages of a life cycle. There is the stage of early detection and prevention. There is the long middle stage of curative treatment, and there is the last stage of death and burial. A

Somali friend once aptly remarked to a group that "the eggshell of Somali unity is now broken. We may talk about making a scrambled egg or an omelet out of it, but we cannot reconstitute the original broken shell!" Treating the problems that led to the separation was possible during the early and middle stages, but not now.

Second, this separation is not the result of manipulation by few politicians. Some people confuse the declaration of the Republic of Somaliland by the SNM in Burao on May 18, 1991 with the fact of separation itself. Separation was a political reality long before that. It is a consequence of an historical process whose two protagonists were the cruel persecution by the regime and the stubborn resistance of the persecuted. It is the culmination of the victory of that lonely struggle by the SNM for an extended period. Siyad Barre himself effectively sanctioned the separation and put the last nail on the coffin of the union y his bombardment of the cities of the north and the mass murder of their citizens which led to the fleeing of terrorized civilians into Ethiopia.

To ignore the victory, which to them is not only the downfall of the Siyad Barre regime, but also includes the separation itself, won by the people of Somaliland with such superhuman sacrifice, or to treat it as non-existent, is foolhardy and borders on the callous. The Burao declaration only put the final touches on an already existing reality.

Third, the present use of "Somali unity" is a misnomer. The original meaning of unity for the Post World War II Somali independence movement was the liberation of the five parts into which the Somali-speaking peoples were divided by the colonial powers and their eventual inclusion under one nation state. When the Somaliland Protectorate gained its independence from Britain it had closer and more advantageous links with Djibouti and eastern Ethiopia than it did with Mogadishu. But it chose to sacrifice its newly won statehood and join the Trusteeship territory, without conditions, in order to lay the basis of the united state which the remaining three parts could later join. It is a well-known story how that Somali irredentism collided with the then existing international order, specifically how the neighboring countries and the Organization of African Unity, with the support of the rest of the international system, resisted any notion of revision of African boundaries on the basis of ethnicity. It is common knowledge how the pursuit of their goal of unity by the Somalis and the resistance of their neighbors to that goal caused instability in the Horn, including two major wars between the Somali Republic and Ethiopia, and the introduction of superpower competition and the arms race into the area, to the detriment of their peoples, especially the Somali people who, on all sides, bore the greater brunt of the havoc.

The upshot was the frustration of Somali unity, with Djibouti opting for its separate statehood and the borders with Ethiopia and Kenya remaining intact as left by the colonial powers. The marriage between the two original parts had became unworkable. Some of the reasons were touched upon in this presentation. Rather, the marriage had lost its raison d'etre. After great suffering and with Herculean efforts the people of Somaliland have restored the statehood which they both won and sacrificed in 1960. Moreover, they are willing to go about it through the internationally agreed methods of elections and plebiscites, even though they are by all logic entitled to it. What is indeed strange is that the international community -- as represented by the UN and other regional organizations -- which originally frustrated the Somali unity project, is now opposing the exercise of this legitimate right of self-determination and attempting to maintain and enforce an unworkable marriage and reconciliation and a now non-existent Somali unity.

Fourth, any process of reconciliation requires negotiation and dialogue between existing entities. The state of Somaliland, even though weak and not yet recognized by the international system is a de facto entity brought into existence by its own people. There is no such comparable entity in the south, i.e., the former Trusteeship territory, with which it can negotiate. Even the many factions have no legitimate standing (at least the majority of them) vis-a-vis the peoples they claim to represent in terms of democratic procedure. The proper course, dictated both by logic and justice, is to accept and assist the correct process of political development in Somaliland, while at the same time, encourage similar processes in the south until such time that a comparable entity appears with whom proper negotiations can take place. But, alas, we know this is not the policy at present pursued by the UN. Instead, it is following a policy of strangling Somaliland and enforcing the: establishment of an artificial so-called" government of unity." It is a dead- end with more negative consequences and precious time lost.

In this analysis, I did not follow that beaten path with no exit. Instead, I chose to go beyond and beneath these superficial formulae. There is a Somali proverb -- "Haani guntay ka tolantaa" - which literally means "a vessel is mended from the base upwards," but which can be roughly translated as "charity begins at home." In the spirit of this proverb, my approach was to understand what happened to the Somali way of living. The research and analysis required to reach this understanding is tremendous and lies before all of us. Yet from these simple reflections, one reaches the inescapable conclusion: that what happened is not a matter of an enigmatic primitive society gone astray. Neither is it a question of "warlord" versus chiefs. It is a matter of a system of governance that has gotten off on an early false start since the colonial days and ended up awry with the military dictatorship. The antidote to that system is its antithesis: an antithesis that can only be found through the practical activity of the people, enlightened by some vision.

I have tried to show the contents of that antithesis as well as the vision in the struggle of the SNM. What we need most urgently is to find ways of resewing the torn fabric of Somali society. Whether that resewn fabric is reconstituted under a single, two, or several states is for a free people to decide. But let us first build that freedom, not on shifting sand, but on solid ground. This is the road for sound reconciliation. And in this respect, the struggle of the SNM, and the present democratic experimentation in Somaliland, have something to offer. We are also willing to learn. But I doubt whether many in the arrogance-ridden UN system and the parrot-like singers of so-called unity in the south are really listening.

APPENDIX

References and extented bibliography on Somaliland

Jama Musse Jama

Abdi, M., N. Osman, S. Tani, U. Terlinden and J. Stockbrügger, 2008, No More 'Grass Grown by the Spear': Addressing Land-based Conflicts in Somaliland, Hargeisa: Academy for Peace and Development.

Abokor, A.Y. and S. Kibble, 2005, Further Steps to Democracy: The Somaliland Parliamentary Elections, September 2005. London: Progressio.

Adam Hussein, 1994, Formation and Recognition of New States: Somaliland in Contrast to Eritrea, Review of African Political Economy, No. 59, Vol. 2.

Africa Watch, 1990, Somalia: A Government at War with its Own People, Africa Watch Committee, New York.

African Union Commission, 2005, Resume: AU Fact-Finding Mission to Somaliland (30 April to 4 May 2005).

Agaloglou, M., 2011, Somaliland: past, Present and Future. Think Africa Press, Part 10, (retrieved April 2011), http://thinkafricapress. com/somalia/somaliland-past-present-and-future-part-10

Ahmed, Sadia M.; Ali, Hassan M.; and Wasame, Amina M., 2001, Report on Research Finding on the State of Pastoralism in Somaliland, (PENHA and ICD), Hargeisa, Somailand.

Ahmed Ismail I., 2000, Remittances and Their Economic Impact in Post-war Somaliland, Disasters 24(4): 380-389.

Ahmed, Ismail I., 1999, The heritage of war and state collapse in Somalia and Somaliland: Local-level effects, external interventions and reconstruction, Third World Quarterly, Vol. 20, No. 1, pp:113 – 127.

Ambroso, G., 2002, Pastoral Society and Ttransnational Refugees: Population Movements in Somaliland and Eastern Ethiopia 1988-2000, New Issues in Refugee Research No.65. Geneva: UNHCR

APD (Academy for Peace and Development), 2004a, Socio-economic Survey 2004 Somaliland. Hargeisa: APD.

APD (Academy for Peace and Development), 2004b, Analysis of Macro-economic Situation in Somaliland, 2004b, Niarobi: UNDP Somalia Watching Brief.

Bayart, Jean-François, Stephen, Ellis, and Béatrice, Hibou, 1999, The Criminalization of the State in Africa, Oxford: James Currey

Bayne, E.A. Brinkmanship on the Horn: Somali Irredentism Remains a Perilous Factor in Eastern Africa, 1963, American Universities Field Staff.

Bradbury, Mark, 2008, Becoming Somaliland. Oxford: James Currey.

Bradbury, Mark, A.Y. Abokor and A.H. Yusuf, 2003, Somaliland: Choosing Politics Over Violence, Review of African Political Economy 97: 455-478.

Bryden, Matt, 2004, Somalia and Somaliland: Envisioning a Dialogue on the Question of Somali Unity, African Security Review, Vol. 13, No. 2, pp:23-33.

Cabdi, S.I., 2005, The Impact of the War on the Family, in WSP (ed.) Rebuilding Somaliland: Issues and Possibilities, Asmara: The Red Sea Press, pp.269-326.

Cindy F. Holleman, 2002, The Socio-economic Implications of the Livestock Ban in Somaliland, Nairobi: USAID (available: http://pdf.usaid.gov/pdf_docs/PNADJ083.pdf).

Carson Johnnie, 2010, Asst. Secretary Johnnie Carson's Briefing in New York on Africa, Assistant Secretary for African Affairs, U.S. Department of State, Washington DC (24 September).

Drysdale John, 2000, Stoics Without Pillows, London: Haan Associates.

Drysdale John, 1991, Somaliland: The Anatomy of Secession, London: Haan Associates.

EC (European Commission), European Commission Strategy for the Implementation of Special Aid to Somalia 2002-2007. 2002, European Commission, Brussels

Farah, A.Y., 1995, Prospects for peaceful solution to the conflict in "Somaliland". Briefing prepared 25 October, Addis Ababa: UNDP.

Gaani, M.X., 2005, Regulating the Livestock Economy of Somaliland, in WSP (ed.), Rebuilding Somaliland: Issues and Possibilities, Asmara: Red Sea Press, pp.189-268

Hammond, L., 2009, The Absent but Active Constituency: The Role of the Somaliland UK community in Election Politics, Unpublished paper.

Hargeisa Municipality, 2003, Hargeisa Municipality Statistical Abstract, Hargeisa: Hargeisa Municipality.

Hashi, Ahmed Mohammed, 1996, Pastoral livelihood Systems, Resource Trends and Dynamics of local Social Organisations in Sool and Sanag Regions: Main Report of a Pastoral Insitutional Survey, (VETAID, UK), Draft, October 1996.

Hashi, Ahmed Mohammed, 2001, Import Bans on Somali Livestock by the Gulf Countries: Justifications for and efforts to lift the bans and restore Somali livestock exports, in Somali Studies International Association, 8th International Congress of Somali Studies on "Peace, Governance and Reconstruction," Hargeisa, Somaliland, July 3-13, 2001.

Hoehne, Markus Virgil; Dereje Feyissa and Mahdi Abdil 2011. Comparing Somali and Ethiopian diasporic engagement for peace in the Horn of Africa. African Conflict & Peacebuilding Review 1(1): 71-99.

Hoehne, Markus Virgil 2010. L'État de facto du Somaliland. Politique Africaine no. 120: 175-199.

Hoehne, Markus Virgil 2010. Diasporisches Handeln in Bürgerkrieg und Wiederaufbau: Beispiele aus Somalia und Somaliland. Friedens-Warte 85(1-2): 83-103.

Hoehne, Markus Virgil 2009. Mimesis and mimicry in dynamics of state and identity formation in northern Somalia. Africa 79(2): 252-281.

Hoehne, Markus Virgil 2011. Education and peacebuilding in post-conflict Somaliland: the role ofthe diaspora. In Joschka Philipps, Kerstin Priwitzer and Heribert Weiland (eds) Education in Fragile Contexts. Freiburg i. Br.: Arnold-Bergstraesser-Institut 2010 (Freiburger Beiträge zu Entwicklung und Politik).

Hoehne, Markus Virgil Forthcoming. Die somalische Diaspora: Rollen und Chancen in (Bürger-)Krieg und Wiederaufbau. In Walter Feichtinger und Gerald Hainzl (eds), Somalia: Optionen - Chancen – Stolpersteine. Frankfurt/M, Weimar: Böhlau.

Hoehne, Markus Virgil 2011. Not born a de facto state: the complicated state formation of Somaliland. In Berouk Mesfin (ed.), Regional Security in the Post-Cold War Horn of Africa. Addis Ababa: ISS.

Hoehne, Markus Virgil and Dereje Feyissa, 2010, State Borders and Borderlands as Resources: An Analytical Framework. In Dereje Feyissa and Markus V. Hoehne (eds.), Borders and borderlands as Resources in the Horn of Africa. London: James Currey, pp. 1-25.

Hoehne, Markus Virgil, 2010, People and Politics along and across the Somaliland-Puntland Border. In Dereje Feyissa and Markus V. Hoehn (eds.), Borders and borderlands as Resources in the Horn of Africa. London: James Currey, pp. 97-121.

Hoehne, Markus Virgil 2010. Somaliland. Un estado de facto en el Cuerno de África. In Jordi Tomas (ed.), Secesionismo en África, Edicions Bellaterra: Barcelona, pp. 365-404.

Hoehne, Markus Virgil and Virginia Luling 2010. Introduction: Lewis and the remaining challenges in Somali Studies. In Markus V. Hoehne and Virginia Luling (eds.), Milk and peace, drought and war: Somali culture, society and politics (Essays in honour of I.M. Lewis). London: Hurst, pp 1-15.

Hoehne, Markus Virgil; Muuse Cali Faruur and Axmed Cabdullahi Du'aale 2010. Somali (nick)names and their meanings. In Markus V. Hoehne and Virginia Luling (eds.), Milk and peace, drought and war: Somali culture, society and politics (Essays in honour of I.M. Lewis). London: Hurst, pp. 345-363.

Hoehne, Markus Virgil 2010. Political representation in Somalia: citizenship, clanism and territoriality. In Mark Bradbury and Sally Healy (eds.), Accord 21: Whose peace is it anyway? connecting Somali and international peacemaking, pp. 34-37.

Hoehne, Markus Virgil; Dereje Feyissa, Mahdi Abdile, and Clara Schmitz-Pranghe, 2010, Differentiating the Diaspora: Reflections on diasporic engagement 'for peace' in the Horn of Africa. Working Paper 124. Halle/Saale: Max Planck Institute for Social Anthropology.

Hoehne, Markus Virgil 2010. Diasporic engagement in the educational sector in post-conflict Somaliland: A contribution to peacebuilding? Diaspeace Working Paper No. 5.

ICG (International Crisis Group), 2006, Somaliland: Time for African Union Leadership Africa Report, No. 110.

ICG (International Crisis Group), 2003, Somaliland: Democratisation and its Discontents. Africa Report No. 66. ICG, Nairobi/Brussels.

Jama Musse Jama, 2002, A note on "My teachers' group": News report of an injustice, Ponte Invisibile, Pisa.

Jhazbhay, Iqbal, (2012) (forthcoming), Terrorism and Counter-Terrorism in Somalia and Somaliland in Anneli Botha, Terrorism in Africa, Institute for Security Studies.

Jhazbhay, Iqbal, 2010, An Approach towards understanding Somaliland's post-war nation-building and international relations", Politeia, Vol. 28, 20-41.

Jhazbhay, Iqbal, 2010, Political Islam, Africa, and the 'War on Terror': Engaging African & US Interests in Melinda Smith, Securing Africa, 9/11 and the Discourse on Terrorism, Ashgate Publishing Ltd, UK.

Jhazbhay, Iqbal, 2010, Somaliland's case of successful power sharing: An Islamic-traditional pact & lessons learnt in Cornelius Du Toit, Power sharing and African Democracy: Interdisciplinary perspectives. Tshwane: Unisa Research Institute for Theology and Religion 173-15

Jhazbhay, Iqbal, 2009, Somaliland Quo Vadis: Overcoming Africa's Post Colonial Self- determination Conundrum (1991-2006), African Historical Review, June, 1-50.

Jhazbhay, Iqbal, 2009, Somaliland: An African Struggle for Nationhood and International Recognition. Johannesburg: Institute for Global Dialogue & South African Institute of International Affairs.

Jhazbhay, Iqbal, 2009, Somaliland: The journey of resistance, reconciliation and peace, African Safety Promotion, Vol. 7 (1), 50-76.

Jhazbhay, Iqbal, 2008, Islam and Stability in Somaliland and the Geo-politics of the War on Terror, Journal of Muslim Minority Affairs, Vol. 28, No. 2, August (2008), 173-205.

Jhazbhay, Iqbal, 2008, Somaliland's Post-War Reconstruction: Rubble to rebuilding in International Journal of African Renaissance Studies, Volume 3 (1) (2008), 59-93.

Jhazbhay, Iqbal, 2008, Somaliland's Post War Nation-Building & Geo-Politics: Lessons Learned in Peace-Building in John Mackinlay, Terrence Mc Namee and Greg Mills, International Peace-Building for the 21st Century: Tswalu Protocol and Background Papers, London: Royal United Services Institute, 189-199.

Jhazbhay, Iqbal, 2006, African Union and Somaliland: Time to Affirm 'Africa's Best-Kept Secret'?, Sub-Saharan Informer, Addis Ababa, 17 March (2006).

Jhazbhay, Iqbal, 2006, Somaliland has strong case for recognition, Sudan Tribune, 2 April (2006) & Sunday Independent, 2 April (2006).

Jhazbhay, Iqbal, 2006, ETHIOPIA, SOMALILAND & SOMALIA AMID AN ISLAMIST RISING STORM ON THE HORN: The African Union & the Case for Urgent Preventive Diplomacy, Centre for Policy Studies, Policy: issues and actors, volume 19, no 8 (December 2006) 1-44.

Jhazbhay, Iqbal, 2004, African Security Review on Horn of Africa (Sudan, Somaliland, Somalia), and Editorial, "Horn of Hope", Volume 13 (2), 1-3.

Jhazbhay, Iqbal, 2003, Somaliland: Africa's best kept secret, A Challenge to the international community?, African Security Review, 12 (4) (2003), 77-82.

Jhazbhay, Iqbal, 2003, Somaliland Success: Africa's Big Secret, Arab News, Saudi Arabia, 29 July (2003).

Kahin, Dalmar, a collection of articles on Somaliland. Available at http://www.americanchronicle.com/authors/view/4458 (retreived 27 April 2011).

Kibble, S. and A.Y. Abokor, 2006, Thoughts on Elections and Post-elections: a Somaliland/UK Civil Society Perspective, Paper presented at SOPRI 2nd Somaliland Convention, 'The Governance and Economic Development of Somaliland', Washington, DC, 8-10 September

King, A., 2003, Hargeisa Urban Household Economy Assessment February-March 2003. Hargeisa: FEWS Net.

Kleist, N. and P. Hansen, 2007, Performing Diaspora: The Mobilization of a Somaliland Transborder Citizenry in A. Osman Farah, M. Muchie, and J. Gundel (eds), Somalia: Diaspora and State Reconstitution in the Horn of Africa. London: Adonis & Abbey, pp. 114-134

Laitin, D. and S. Samatar, 1988, Somalia - Nation in Search of a State, London: Gower.

Lewis, I.M., 2002, A Modern History of Somalia - Nation and State in the Horn of Africa, 2002, 4th Ed., London: Longman.

Lewis, I.M., 1989, The Ogaden and the Fragility of Somali Segmentary Nationalism, African Affairs 88: 573-579.

Lewis, I.M., 1994, Blood and Bone: The Call of Kinship in Somali Society. Lawrenceville, NJ: Red Sea Press.

Lewis, I. M., 1972, The Politics of the 1969 Somali Coup, The Journal of Modern African Studies, Vol. 10, No. 3, pp:383-408.

Lewis, I.M., 1961, A Pastoral Democracy, 1961, London: Oxford University Press.

Lindley, A., 2010, The Early Morning Phonecall: Somali Refugees' Remittances, Oxford: Berghahn Books.

Lindley, A., 2010, Seeking refuge in an unrecognized state: Oromos in Somaliland, Refuge, 26(1): 187-189.

Lindley, A., 2010, Leaving Mogadishu: Towards a Sociology of Conflict-Related Migration, Journal of Refugee Studies, 23(1): 2-22.

Lindley, A., 2010, The North-South Divide in Everyday Life: Somali Londoners Sending Money "Home", Bildhaan: An International Journal of Somali Studies, 9: 39-62.

Lindley, A., 2009, Between "Dirty Money" and "Development Capital": Somali Money Transfer Infrastructure Under Global Scrutiny, African Affairs 108(433): 519-539.

Lindley, A., 2009, The Early Morning Phonecall: Remittances from a Refugee Diaspora Perspective, Journal of Ethnic and Migration Studies 35(8): 1315-1334.

Lindley, A., 2008, Transnational Connections and Education in the Somali Context, Journal of Eastern African Studies 2(2): 404-414.

Lindley, A., 2006, Migration and Financial Transfers: UK-Somalia, Refuge, 23(1): 20-27.

Rajagopal, B. and Carroll, A. J., The Case for the Independent Statehood of Somaliland. American University Journal of International Law & Policy, Vol. 8.

Scoones Ian, et al., 2010, Zimbabwe's Land Reform: Myths & Realities, James Currey, Woodbridge.

Somaliland Centre for Peace and Development, 2001, Self-Portrait of Somaliland, (WSP), Hargeysa.

Somaliland Centre for Peace and Development, Regulating the Livestock Economy, (WSP), forthcoming.

Somaliland Chamber of Commerce, 2004, Somaliland Trade Directory, Hargeysa: Somaliland Chamber of Commerce.

Somaliland Policy and Reconstruction Institute (SOPRI), 2006, Planning document, http://www.sopri.org/delegation_info.pdf accessed 21 April 2011.

Spears, I. S., 2004, Debating Secession and the Recognition of New States in Africa, African Security Review, Vol. 13, No. 2, pp:35-48.

Touval S., 1963, Somali Nationalism – International Politics and the Drive for Unity in the Horn of Africa, Cambridge: Harward University Press.

Tripodi, P., 1999, The Colonial Legacy in Somalia: Rome and Mogadishu: from Colonial Administration to Operation Restore Hope, New York: St. Martin's Press.

Walls, Michael and Kibble, Steve, 2010, 'Identity, Stability and the State in Somaliland: Indigenous Forms and External Interventions', paper presented to the Globalisation(s) of the Conflict in Somalia conference (24-25 March), St Andrews: University of St Andrews.

Walls, Michael and Kibble, Steve, 2010, Beyond Polarity: Negotiating a Hybrid State in Somaliland, in: Africa Spectrum, 45, 1, 31-56.

Yannis, A., 2000, State Collapse and the International System – Implosion of Government and the International Legal Order from the French Revolution to the Disintegration of Somalia, Geneva: IUHEI.

NOTES ON THE CONTRIBUTORS

Mohamed A Omar
Somaliland Foreign Affairs and International Cooperation Minister, Mohamed A Omar (PhD) is academic, writer and political analyst with special interest in African politics, post-conflict state reconstruction and international relations.

Sylvie Aboa-Bradwell
Founder and director of the African Peoples Advocacy (APA, www. apadvocacy.org). Before founding APA in 2008, she worked for several years as UK co-ordinator of the Centre for Democracy and Development, and for various non-governmental organisations in Spain.

Abdishakur Jowhar
Abdishakur Jowhar is a medical doctor and a specialist in Psychiatry. He lives in Hargaysa, Somaliland for 6 months of the year where he runs a psychiatric clinic and he runs a similar clinic in Ontario, Canada for the other 6 months of the year.

Michael Walls
Lecturer and Course Co-Director of MSc Development Administration and Planning at University College London (UCL). His research, consultancy and teaching interests lie in the related areas of development management and governance, including doctoral research in political governance in Somaliland. Dr. Walls is actively involved in a number of groups, including the Anglo-Somali Society, Somaliland Focus (UK) and Kayd Somali Arts and Culture Ltd, and he was one of the joint coordinators of the 26 June 2010 Somaliland presidential international election observers.

Steve Kibble
Policy and Advocacy Coordinator – Africa, Middle East and Asia for the international development agency Progressio, Dr. Kibble holds a

doctorate in African politics from the University of Leeds. He lobbies and writes extensively on Southern and Eastern African politics and, with Michael Walls, he was one of the joint coordinators of the 26 June 2010 Somaliland presidential international election observers.

Ibrahim Megag Samater
A former Planning Minister for Somali Republic, Ibrahim Megag Samatar was a Cabinet member of the Siyad Barre regime for nine years and then his Ambassador in Bonne for one year. He eventually defected and sought asylum in the United States. He joined the SNM and became the chairman of their Central Committee and Chair of the interim national assembly in Somaliland.

Editor
Jama Musse Jama, a mathematician by formation, now works as an IT Senior Anlyst in the telecomunication industry. He is the founding president of redsea-online.com Cultural Foundation and Editor in chief of its publishing arm, Ponte Invisibile Ed. He is the author, among others, of "A note on my teachers' group: news report on injustice" and "Gobannimo bilaash maaha" (freedom is not free).

Printed in the United States
By Bookmasters